STEVENS PASS

The Story of Railroading and Recreation in the North Cascades

STEVENS PASS

The Story of Railroading and Recreation in the North Cascades

JoAnn Roe

THE
MOUNTAINEERS

Published by The Mountaineers
1011 SW Klickitat Way
Seattle, Washington 98134
U.S.A.

9 8 7 6 5
5 4 3 2 1

Published simultaneously in Canada by Douglas & McIntyre, Ltd., 1615 Venables Street, Vancouver, B.C. V5L 2H1

Published simultaneously in Great Britain by Cordee, 3a DeMontfort Street, Leicester, England, LE1 7HD

Manufactured in the United States of America

Edited by Sherri Schultz
Drawings and maps by Newell Cartographics
Cover design by Dorothy Wachtenheim Design
Book design and typesetting by The Mountaineers Books
Book layout by Word Graphics

Cover photographs courtesy of Special Collections Division, University of Washington Libraries: *top*, driving under difficulties—first return trip from Index over county road (neg. Pickett 1411); *bottom*, train along Tumwater Canyon, Leavenworth, Washington (neg. 13656)
Frontispiece: Electronic locomotive used to pull trains over Stevens Pass

Library of Congress Cataloging-in-Publication Data
Roe, JoAnn
    Stevens Pass : the story of railroading and recreation in the North
  Cascades / JoAnn Roe.
       p. cm.
    Includes index.
    ISBN 0-89886-371-6
    1. Stevens Pass (Wash.)—History. 2. Railroads—Washington
  (State)—Stevens Pass—History. 3. Outdoor recreation—Washington
  (State)—Stevens Pass—History. I. Title.
F897.C3R62   1995
917.97'59—dc20   95-7509
                                                    CIP

Contents

Preface

Stevens Pass has always had an aura of mystery about it. It was not discovered as a practical pass until the late 1800s; even the Indians preferred Cady Pass as a trail from east to west. Hot springs emanated from several spots on the west side of Stevens Pass, hinting of past volcanic activity. Awesome snowfalls, the very element that makes the ski areas of the pass attractive today, scythed down lives in early days. Those who braved the area had to cope with avalanches, dark and towering forests where one could easily become lost, and unforgiving precipices in the alpine regions.

In the half of Washington state that lies north of Snoqualmie Pass, there was no practical road across the Cascade Range until 1951, when the state finally accepted responsibility for the highway across Stevens Pass. True, the Cascade Scenic Highway opened (in good weather only) in 1925, but it was more of a trail, only fourteen feet wide in places and boggy on the west side. The railroad was the star of the setting, lending "romance" to the crossing, though its real saga consisted of the blood, sweat, and tears of brawny construction crews, ghastly design mistakes, and cruel acts of nature no one could predict—as well as the determination of courageous magnates, through trial and error and despite countless obstacles, to lay tracks between communities.

Yet individuals traversed the mountains, built crude homes, raised their children, and schooled them at home or in drafty log schoolhouses with few books. Nefarious pioneers took advantage of the isolation to work scams, fight, steal, and even murder.

The story of Stevens Pass is a story of the frontier. It is a different kind of frontier from the Wild West, but it parallels that other frontier, for its brave pioneers lived on the edges of lightly populated, barely civilized settlements along Puget Sound and in the Spokane-Boise area. Good and bad, it is the story of our own beginnings in the Pacific Northwest mountain country.

Acknowledgments

I would like to thank Ralph Newell for taking me to the Trinity Mine; Lloyd Berry for lending me copies of railroad surveys; Elaine Berry for lending me Chris Rogers' paper on the Icicle Irrigation Project; Ruth Norton for making available her unpublished manuscript on the history of Skykomish; James Moore of the Washington State Archives, Northwest Region, for research assistance; Grant Sharpe for suggested references; Peter Thompson of the Great Northern Railway Historical Society for suggested sources; Glen Katzenberger for sharing his files and scrapbook, and for numerous consultations on Stevens Pass history; Willie Jones for reading my completed manuscript on railroad matters; John Brown for a reading of Indian history; Jan Hollenbeck of the U.S. Forest Service for valuable suggestions; Chelan County Historical Museum for consultations; Ruth Ittner for lending me The Mountaineers scrapbooks; Mark Behler of the North Central Washington Museum for conferences; the *Wenatchee World* and Hu Blonk for use of great amounts of reference material from the newspaper; the staff of the Bellingham Public Library for their patient handling of requests for microfilm and material from outside sources; the staff of the Special Collections, Allen Library, University of Washington; the staff of The Mountaineers Books for their confidence that I could ferret out and assemble from such diverse sources a readable account of Stevens Pass; and Sherri Schultz, the editor, for her careful scrutiny of all aspects of the manuscript for accuracy.

I am particularly indebted to the individuals listed below for the information provided to me through oral interviews:

Jim Adamson, Hermod Bakke, John Brown, Marilyn and LeRoy Carter, Byron Dickinson, Ramona Dudek, Ann Fink, Franz Gabl, Jim George, Lloyd Hill, Willie Jones, Thelma Kasophous, Glen Katzenberger, Bruce Kehr, Louise Lindgren, Paul and Kathleen Mankin, Dennis McMillin, Pat Morris, Ralph Newell, William Newell, Ruth and Bob Norton, Delwyn Nowak, Tom Olson, Mary and Arthur Ren, Ian Richey, Margaret Smith, Claude Thomson, William Thorson, Joyce and James Wilson Timpe, Norman Trapp, John Ware, and Pauline Watson.

Introduction

Warmly clad in the products of technology, our waterproof boots and scientifically designed hiking equipment protecting us from the elements, we must marvel at the travails of early explorers and workers.

Over the last twenty-five years, I have hiked, ridden horses, slept in the snow, and been drenched by sudden rains in Washington's rugged Cascades, an impressive range boasting a consistent array of snow-covered peaks of around 8,000 feet, punctuated by volcanic cones that soar 10,000 to 14,500 feet. As a writer of popular history, I often mentally placed myself in those mountains a century earlier. What would I have experienced? Why would I have endured the dangers? Some pioneers of the region gave their names to local landmarks; others left us their diaries and tales. From these sources and the fine research of scholars using historical documents and political records, we can relive the settlers' adventures.

The state of Washington is a singular place, often little understood by the outsider. Tucked in the northwestern corner of the United States, bisected neatly into eastern and western halves by the towering peaks of the North Cascades, the state has two distinct faces. Much of the state's eastern half is arid, flat, and treeless. Carved into the plain are starkly beautiful canyons. The western half has ample rain that falls mostly during the six months of fall and winter, making the land lush and green. It is indented by complex saltwater bays and coves and supplied by rivers tumbling musically from the mountains. Today the eastern half is also green, well watered from irrigation systems linked mostly to the vast Columbia River watershed.

Washington's geologic history is spellbinding. On the western side of the state, glaciers once pushed southward from Canada to a point south of Seattle, lying as much as 5,000 feet deep over today's city of Bellingham. (Today one can see "high-water" marks along such North Cascades peaks as Church Mountain.) As the earth warmed and glaciers melted, the water filled a series of lakes lying between Vancouver and Seattle until they overflowed and merged with the Pacific through the Strait of Juan de Fuca. Puget Sound became an arm of the Pacific and, within the Sound, only the tops of small mountains stayed above water, becoming islands.

At least three-quarters of the eastern half of Washington was built by the repeated upwelling of lava, which congealed into a huge volcanic plain. At Vantage, on the Columbia River, one can see the petrified remains of exotic tropical trees that were overwhelmed by lava and water. No wonder that the plain is so fertile today; it is pulverized volcanic soil. Later in geologic time, glaciers pushed southward to block the ancient riverbed of the Columbia River at Bridgeport (west of Grand Coulee Dam) and spill over onto the volcanic plains near Mansfield. That glacier did not melt as quickly as some farther east, above Spokane and near Missoula, Montana. When an ice dam at Lake Missoula fractured, torrents of water raced into the old Columbia River bed, slammed against the unmelted glacier covering Bridgeport's site, and were shunted southward. The raging water ripped out the dramatic Grand Coulee, Sun Lakes, and other coulees through natural faults. The cataclysm was repeated several times. Eventually the Columbia returned to its present-day bed.

Prevented by the terrain from frequent contact with their neighbors, the state's native people tended to live in cloistered communities—in the west deriving their living from the sea, in the east from hunting and fishing. Periodically, they met to exchange products at The Dalles, Oregon.

Discouraged by the harsh geography of Washington, the first explorers and settlers came from the sea, too. Europeans and Americans sailed from the Atlantic Ocean into the Pacific around Cape Horn or through the Strait of Magellan in the 1700s and 1800s. Bound for Cathay in swift clipper ships, merchants sped to trade with the Orient. Sturdy, smelly whaling ships thrust northwesterly toward the Asian coast with crews in pursuit of whales, first stopping in the South Sea islands to give the storm-tossed men respite.

Few ships battled along America's Northwest coast, however, until the search began for the Northwest Passage, a fabled opening that would permit ships to pass through the American land mass and thus reduce sailing time to the Orient. Persistent rumors of a mighty passage led men such as James Cook and George Vancouver, two of the principal explorers of the Northwest, to search along what is now the Oregon-Washington coast. But it was an American, Captain Robert Gray, who discovered the mouth of the Columbia River in 1792, a feat that became a hook on which the U.S. government hung its claim to today's state of Washington.

The Hudson's Bay Company had trappers in today's northern British Columbia as early as the 1600s, but it was not until 1811 that the origin of the 1,214-mile Columbia River, south of Banff, was discovered—by former Hudson's Bay surveyor David Thompson, then in the employ of the North West Company. Having purchased Fort Astoria from the United States during the War of 1812, the British-backed Hudson's Bay hastened to build other forts along the Columbia and considered the entire area we now know as Washington state to be its property. The forts were not military facilities but supply and trading posts. Hudson's Bay men traveled by river far north into Canada, and by sea from Fort Vancouver (near Portland) into Puget Sound. Settlers coming to Oregon Territory and, later, to the Washington Territory arrived via the Columbia River and turned south or north, respectively, from Portland.

Supplied by the burgeoning ship traffic, cities grew along the Pacific's inland reaches, the Georgia Strait, Puget Sound, and the rivers. One of the most rapidly growing cities was Seattle, founded in 1851 by a few families and bolstered by the sawmill built by Henry Yesler in 1853. With the discovery of gold at Barkerville, far north of the Canadian border, the towns of Bellingham, Everett, La Conner, and Port Townsend came to life.

Visionaries realized, however, that until the Cascades could be conquered and a railroad built from the east to either the Pacific Ocean or Puget Sound, growth would be limited. In the late 1850s Seattleites hacked out a wagon road through Snoqualmie Pass. The year 1888 marked the extension of the Northern Pacific Railroad (later renamed the Northern Pacific Railway) across nearby Stampede Pass to a terminus at Tacoma, where it connected with a north-south Northern Pacific route.

Railroad fever spread throughout the West during this period. Not only the Northern Pacific but also the Great Northern Railroad had surveyors searching for a more northerly route to Puget Sound so entrepreneurs could cash in on the Orient trade. In 1893, using private capital but in cahoots with lumber conglomerates, James J. Hill completed the Great Northern Railroad, which gave Everett and Seattle direct access to eastern markets and suppliers.

Unquestionably, it was Hill's push to build his railroad that resulted not only in the discovery of Stevens Pass but also in the development of the area's towns and resources. Before the construction of the railroads and the subsequent highways—today there are still only four cross-mountain thoroughfares in almost three hundred miles—Washington stood divided into two parts.

The task of developing the area was never easy. Forests were so dense that one could not see the sun. Snows of incredible depth choked the western slopes (for the pass invites the entry of storm systems and winds coming from the Pacific). Bitter winter cold marked the eastern side of the mountain range, heavy rains the western coastal lands. The thrust of development was economic at first, but as people came through the North Cascades, they were overwhelmed by the sheer beauty of the place, and so the further explorations of the backcountry began.

THE EAST SIDE:
Early Years

1. LIFE AMONG THE WENATCHI INDIANS

The Wenatchi Indians were the original inhabitants of the area east of Stevens Pass. According to ethnohistorical reports compiled by anthropologist Verne Ray, in the 1850s the Wenatchi villages in the area covered by this book were Alot´as, a permanent village of about 200 on Wenatchee Flats; Ntu´atckam, a winter population of around 400 at the mouth of Mission Creek (now Cashmere); Tcum´aus, a summer village at the junction of the Icicle and Wenatchee rivers; an unnamed camp at the site of today's town of Leavenworth; Tciw´ax, a fishing village of 100 at the confluence of the Chiwawa and Wenatchee rivers; Tcitciw´aux, a small hunting and fishing village at Rock Creek and the Chiwawa River; Tahkwut, a band at Lake Wenatchee led by a chief named Skamow; and three other camps farther south.

Although the Wenatchi Indians were Salish speakers, they mingled closely with the Yakima Indians, a Sahaptin linguistic group, living near and intermarrying with them. These Salish people consisted of several bands, including the Methow, the Chelan, and the Entiat, who like the Wenatchis tended to live along the west bank of the Columbia River and the valleys to the west. Two small related groups, the Siapkat and Camiltpaw, lived southeast of today's town of Wenatchee. Under pressure from southerly Sahaptin bands, the Wenatchis' lands gradually shrank to center largely on the Wenatchee River valley.

Like most eastern Washington tribes, the Wenatchi Indians were seminomadic, moving as far south as Celilo Falls on the Columbia River to fish, hunt, and trade, and occasionally trekking over a Cascades trail to barter with coastal Indians. During spring and fall, families and bands roved northward around Lake Wenatchee or down the Wenatchee River toward today's Cashmere to hunt or dig roots. April was the time for bitterroot on Badger Mountain, east of the Columbia, and midsummer was camas-digging time near Lake Wenatchee. Then came the major salmon catches, a time of socializing as well as hard work. At present-day Leavenworth, where the clear, cold waters of Chumstick, Icicle, and other creeks joined the Wenatchee River, there was a major traditional fishery known as the Wenatshapam. Not only the Wenatchis but more distant, friendly bands such as the Yakima and Okanogan Indians came to the fishery. Some Wenatchis also speared fish or built weirs at the junction of the Wenatchee and the Columbia or at other likely spots when the salmon migrated from the ocean, up the Columbia, and into many spawning streams.

During winter most Wenatchi families retreated downriver to the Cashmere area or to Wenatchee Flats, at the junction of the Wenatchee and the Columbia. Preparations for winter were preceded by a big party, a sort of family reunion. The smoke of campfires carried the aroma of roasting salmon. The valley rang with the laughter of children and adults playing traditional games. A favorite of spectators was a game in which a contestant ran to a container, picked up a large, live salmon, and ran back to the finish line. The slippery salmon would object vigorously, often escaping into the dust before the competitor could manage to recapture it—to the glee of the onlookers.

Fortunes were made and lost on horse racing at Wenatchee Flats. Wagers of goods were made by piling up items until the gamblers agreed on the amount. Restless horses pranced and snorted, anticipating the race to come. Sellers held their horses impassively as potential buyers piled up goods to tempt the sellers. When an offer was satisfactory, a seller would suddenly hand the reins to the new owner and pick up his booty.

In an article for *Century Magazine*, Lieutenant C. E. S. Wood described a race held during an 1879 conference at Wenatchee. It was a match race between two horses, each representing a different tribe and each loyally supported by the respective tribe members:

> Here the horses took their stand, stark naked, save the fine buffalo-hair lariats knotted around their lower jaws. They were little beauties, clean cut as barbs, one a white and the other a gray; the skin fine, the sinews clean and silky, nostrils immense, heads small, bony, necks graceful, slim. . . . By each stood its rider, a young Indian boy, slim and sinewy as

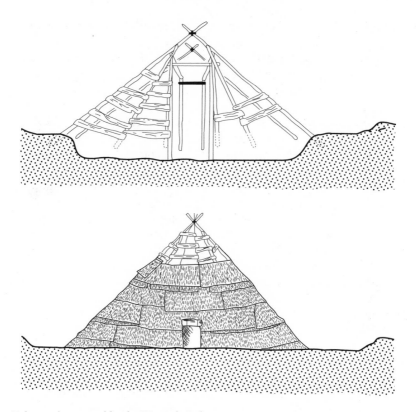

Tule-mat house used by the Wenatchi Indians

his horse, and as naked, save the most meager breech-clout. . . . Crowds began to flock to the stand. The racers were examined . . . to see that all was sound and fair.

Now the betting began, first by the two owners: a saddle and bundle of furs by one, a bundle of blankets by the other. Then the audience bet, making heaps of goods as their wagers or offering as many as ten horses. Finally, within a lane formed by the watchers, the race began:

A faint cry at the other end of the line, a whirl of the horses, a tumult down there, a waving of whips, a wild yelling growing nearer, louder, and here they come—flying. Side by side, the naked riders plying the lash with every terrific bound; . . . Here they come: heads out, eyes strained, nostrils stretched, forehoofs seeming always in the air, the whip-thongs falling with a quickening vigor. A hoarse, wild shouting, a deafening burst of yells, a swish in the air, an apparition before the eyes, a bound over the finish line, and the race is over, the white just half a length ahead.

Preparing for winter was serious business. While the Wenatchis lived all summer in portable homes similar to tepees (but made of crosspoles and tule mats), the harsh winter required better shelter. Family members excavated a spacious circular pit, erected a framework, and added the tule mats, held down by slanted poles.

An extended family group lived in such a pit house, with smoked fish and meat and dried berries hanging from the framework, through the winter. Heavy snows might completely bury the pit house temporarily, winds could whistle sharply above it, and wild animals might sniff hungrily around the rooftops, but the subterranean dwelling was most practical and warm. If sufficient food had been stored and spring did not come late, the family fared well. Babies were born, the elderly died peacefully, and the accumulated knowledge of the tribe was imparted to the young through legends and stories during these relatively inactive times. It was also in winter that the Wenatchi craftsmen, renowned among the region's tribes for excellence, fashioned soapstone pipes, basalt war clubs, and arrow points of precious stones. (In 1987, magnificent fluted points were uncovered in an east Wenatchee orchard, creating great excitement among archaeologists. The artisans are believed to have been members of a prehistoric people that lived in the area 10,000 to 12,000 years ago.)

Until the 1990s, historians believed that the Indians did not often venture into the higher mountains; even the Indian legends seemed to indicate that the Wenatchis were afraid of the spirits in the snowy fastnesses. This belief is being shattered by the frequent discoveries of pit houses in many high-altitude locations in the North Cascades around Stevens Pass and in the Wenatchee and Entiat mountains. Apparently, some families preferred to spend their winters in comparative isolation rather than come down to the flats. (To prevent damage to the remains, archaeologists have not revealed the exact locations of the houses.)

A lifestyle that may have existed for as long as 12,000 years began to change in the early 1800s. During the winter of 1805–06, the Wenatchis' conversations probably included the astonishing news of pale human beings who bore wondrous goods; the explorers Meriwether Lewis and William Clark encountered southerly roaming Wenatchis along the Columbia River near Celilo that winter, and Clark met with Yakima Indians at the junction of the Yakima and Columbia rivers. There, conferring with the Indian elders, Clark drew a crude map of the area, one that included what he called the "Wah na a chee" River. Phonetically he may have gotten the name from the Sahaptin word *winatsa* or the Klickitat word *awenatchila*, both indicating a coming or flowing out (of the mountains).

Six years later David Thompson, the discoverer of the headwaters of the Columbia River, made a voyage from Kettle Falls to Astoria, visiting at Wenatchee Flats with local Indians. In his diary, Thompson speculated that the Wenatchis might not have seen a white man before, noting that one Wenatchi asked to feel the explorer's leg to see if he was real.

Fur trappers and more government-backed explorers began to appear in the area more frequently, especially after the 1825 establishment of Fort Vancouver, the southerly bastion of the Hudson's Bay Company, on the Columbia River. The Columbia became the avenue for supply boats and fast canoes spanning the vast distance between Fort Vancouver and scattered northerly fur posts, as well as the Hudson's Bay Company headquarters at Hudson's Bay (York Factory) and later at Red River Settlement (today's Winnipeg). As early as 1814, there was a rival trading post north of the Indians' Wenatchee Flats winter home, at the confluence of the Okanogan and Columbia rivers.

The fur traders came only to trade and glean furs. They sought amicable relations with the Indians and acquired only enough land for trading posts. Like other eastern Washington Indians, the Wenatchis did not feel threatened. That was about to change.

2. CONFRONTATION

The eastern Washington Indians were relatively friendly to explorers, settlers, and traders, who provided them with fascinating goods. Not long after Fort Vancouver was established, a major leader of the Columbia Indians called Sulktalthscosum (Piece Broken from the Sun, or Half-Sun) carried home to Wenatchee Flats chickens, potatoes, and hogs. The potatoes thrived as a substitute for camas bulbs, although the chickens fell prey to wild animals and the hogs themselves became too wild for comfort. The Columbia Indians and their close relatives, the Wenatchis, soon seized the opportunity to raise cattle and horses to sell to the Hudson's Bay Company traders and early settlers.

It was the surveyors and settlers moving into the area who became worrisome to the Indians. In 1843, a 1,000-person wagon train left Independence, Missouri, with most of the settlers bound for the Willamette Valley of Oregon. They and those who came after them flowed into the Northwest like the rivers they followed, armed and generally regarding Indians as a group to be removed, not cultivated.

Unintentionally, the settlers brought weapons worse than rifles—an array of diseases unknown to the Indians that spread like grass fires throughout the susceptible Washington tribes. Measles epidemics partly fueled the rage that resulted in the infamous 1847 Whitman massacre at Walla Walla, in which missionaries Marcus and Narcissa Whitman, along with twelve other settlers, were killed by Indians. Diseases decimated the powerful Wenatchi bands.

For a time, though, relationships between the native people and the interlopers remained cautiously friendly, despite the disease and the growing traffic on the Columbia River. The newcomers and the natives borrowed bits of culture from each other. According to Richard Scheuerman's student researchers in the book *The Wenatchi Indians*, the natives observed that trading posts raised the British flag each Sunday and lowered it on Monday. Thus, Sunday came to be "known as *Skacheeas* or 'Hanging Up Day,' Monday became *Skeewheeoos* or 'Dropped Day.' Tuesday was *Sasslaskt* or 'Second Day' and so forth." Traders adopted Indian methods of making pemmican and curing salmon. Cured salmon were layered in large baskets, covered with grass, and packed down securely. Bound and tied, the fish would be edible for months.

Some natives were converted to Catholicism by their contacts with Hudson's Bay voyageurs or canoemen and with the roving Jesuit priests who came to Oregon Territory to convert the natives. In 1838, Fathers Francis N. Blanchet and Modeste Demers arrived on Hudson's Bay Company canoes bound for Fort Vancouver, intending to work among the natives and settlers of the Cowlitz and Willamette Valleys. Fathers C. M. Pandosy and Respari (first name unknown) were active in Wenatchi country.

Meanwhile, the leadership of the mid-Columbia bands was changing. The Columbian Sulktalthscosum and his eldest son were killed during separate hunting trips to Blackfoot country. The next son, Quiltenenock, married a daughter of a major Wenatchi chief, Tecolekun, and increasingly began to speak for both groups.

The bands were not many in all. George Gibbs, treaty negotiator for Isaac Stevens, the governor of the Washington Territory, said there were only 550 Wenatchi, Columbia, and Okanogan Indians in 1853. Of those, the Okanogans favored lands along the Okanogan and Columbia rivers, north of the Wenatchis' favored grounds. The fortunes of the Wenatchi and Columbia Indians were more bound up with their cousins, the Yakimas, than with the Okanogans.

Each native tribe kept to its favored places to hunt, fish, and spend the seasons, intermingling with other friendly tribes from time to time but retaining its own tribal identity; yet the Indians did not consider the land itself to be "owned." As settlers came into Washington, the United States began to permit homesteading of certain Northwest lands and sent surveyors to facilitate the pending ownerships. The process frightened and alienated the Indians, perhaps more than any warlike act might have done: how could any person own the earth; didn't all of it belong to the Creator?

Then came the Mullan Road surveyors, who laid out a military road from Fort Walla Walla to Fort Benton on the Missouri River. In 1853, Captain George B. McClellan arrived in the foothills of the Cascades to search for a railroad route through the mountains to the Pacific Coast. Realizing he must attempt to work with the Wenatchi Indians in order to go through their lands, he observed that Quiltenenock was working to become the chief of the Wenatchis. McClellan visited the Wenatchis at their winter grounds at Wenatchee Flats and suggested that it would be wise for the natives to appoint a major leader to negotiate with Governor Stevens, who was also the superintendent of Indian affairs for the U.S. government. McClellan cultivated Quiltenenock, giving him handsome gifts and speaking well of him.

McClellan tried to locate a railroad route through Snoqualmie Pass but lost his way, traveling to Yakima Pass instead. He did not venture far toward the area now known as Stevens Pass, since he was discouraged by Quiltenenock's opinion that there was no practical pass in that area of the mountains. McClellan returned south and west through the Columbia Gorge, then went north to Olympia. His wanderings through eastern Washington produced no tangible information as to trails, although he did mention to his superiors that there were traces of gold in the Wenatchee River and elsewhere along the Columbia. It was an unfortunate observation for the Wenatchis.

Meanwhile, Governor Stevens was attempting to hammer out reservation agreements with one tribe at a time. In 1854, Stevens met with influential Yakima chief Owhi (of the Kittitas area) to ask for a major conference the following year at the Walla Walla council grounds. There Stevens hoped to forge land purchases, make treaties, and arrange for reservations so he and the government could proceed with surveying the land, allocating homesteads, and obtaining railroad rights-of-way.

By this time, Quiltenenock's younger brother Quetalican had married Chief Owhi's daughter, further consolidating the loyalties between the Wenatchi, Columbia, and Yakima Indians. The chiefs of all three tribes were deeply distrustful of the government's motives but agreed to go to the Walla Walla conference. The great Yakima chief Kamiakin was viewed by many whites as being more than willing to go to war.

In his book on the Wenatchis, Richard Scheuerman wrote that the U.S. Army's position was one of "non-interference in Indian affairs east of the Cascades. General Jonathan Wool, commanding the Army of the Pacific from California headquarters, contended that if the nation's

Indian policy had proven anything, it was that the Indians and Whites could not live in each other's presence without inciting bloodshed." He held that only well-defined geographic boundaries could effectively prevent hostilities; and therefore, the territory's entire intermountain region should be declared off limits to White settlement. The politician Stevens could not have disagreed more.

Although extremely uneasy about the critical decisions facing them, most of the Indian leaders did agree to Stevens's proposals, after much jockeying back and forth as to size of reservations, details of monetary payments, location of schools, and other matters. The resultant pact became known as the Yakima Treaty of 1855.

At the momentous conference, the chief spokesman for the Wenatchis was Tecolekun, who asked for a separate Wenatchi Indian reservation in the Wenatchee Valley that would have included the traditional Wenatchi fishing grounds, an area from about Leavenworth to Cashmere. His request was not granted. Instead, the Wenatchis were included in the allocations to the Yakimas and were considered part of that tribe. There was one positive result for the Wenatchis, however; Article X of the treaty, reproduced here from Charles J. Kappler's *Indian Affairs, Laws, and Treaties*, provided for the "Wenatshapam Fishery" reservation:

That there is also reserved and set apart from the lands ceded by this treaty, for the use and benefit of the aforesaid Confederated Tribes and Bands, a tract of land not exceeding in quantity one township of six miles square, situated at the forks of the Pisquouse or Wenatshapam [Wenatchee] River, and known as the "Wenatshapam Fishery," which said reservation shall be surveyed and marked out whenever the President may direct, and be subject to the same provisions and restrictions as other Indian reservations. ["Pisquouse" was the name of the Indians in their own language, but they became known as "Wenatchi," the Sahaptin-language term for them.]

The Yakima Treaty had to be ratified by Congress before it could take effect. Ratification did not take place until March 8, 1859. In the meantime, no one was to interfere with the Indian lands or settle on them. It was estimated that the natives would not have to move their people onto the designated reservations for two to three years.

Gold prospectors and would-be settlers, however, erroneously believed that they could immediately enter all lands not actually lived upon by the natives, as well as all lands not included in the new reservation boundaries—a substantially different interpretation of the treaty than the one held by the Indians. After several disagreements between Indians and miners, tensions rose when an Indian named Mosheel led a group of Yakima Indians, with whom Indian agent A. J. Bolon was traveling, to murder Bolon without apparent provocation in October 1855. Mosheel's father, Showawai Kotiaken (also called Ice), was said to have cried when he learned of the deed.

Much magnified by the press, the murder caused the area's settlers to panic, fearing general Indian uprisings. The Army was encouraged to act. Major Granville Haller, with over a hundred men, lost a skirmish against the Indians near Toppenish. At Union Gap about a month later, a major army of 850 troopers, led by Major Gabriel Rains and Lieutenant Phil Sheridan, scattered the resisting Indians. Some fled over the snowy Wenatchee Mountains to refuge in the valley of Leavenworth.

In May 1856, Colonel George Wright set up camp in the Naches River valley and asked the leaders of the opposition to surrender. No one came. Wright decided to root out the guilty and the leaders of bands talking war, who he had heard were living among the Wenatchis. On July 6, Wright came into the valley along Peshastin Creek, essentially along today's Blewett Pass highway, toward the Wenatshapam fishery. Learning of his approach, many of the hunted fled back east across the Columbia—including Kamiakin and Owhi, even though the latter, accompanied by Quiltenenock and Quetalican, had earlier come to Wright to express a willingness to talk peace.

At the fishery, Skamow, an influential Wenatchi leader who usually lived in the upper Wenatchee Valley, told Wright that he had heard that Tecolekun had received a reservation that included the fishery. He asked Wright for a letter of confirmation, which Skamow then reportedly wore as a talisman in a pouch around his waist for years. Father C. M. Pandosy, a Jesuit who had been working among the Wenatchis, also acted as an intermediary for the local people, assuring Wright that they had no warlike intent.

Presuming that peace had been established, Wright and his troopers escorted the suspected murderers of Bolon, as well as many displaced Yakimas living among the Wenatchis near Leavenworth, back to the Kittitas Valley and beyond. His path this time took the party down the south bank of the Wenatchee to the Columbia and from there to the Yakima River. The column of people, horses, and possessions extended for five miles.

The peace was uneasy, partly because of the power struggle between the Army under Wright and the citizens volunteer army permitted to operate independently in the same area by Governor Stevens. The volunteer army was an ill-equipped, poorly led group that had been hastily organized after the Bolon murder. It was accused of depredations suggestive of a band of outlaws—for example, attacking innocent Indian families at random. In this unsettled situation, General Wool ordered

Isaac Stevens, first governor of Washington Territory, who negotiated many northwest Indian treaties (Photo: Washington State Historical Society, Tacoma, WA)

Wright to blockade any further white settlers from the area, which effectively dismantled the volunteer forces.

Although the friction between Stevens and the Army continued, and Stevens eventually used his political clout in Washington, D.C. to replace General Wool, it was the continuing intemperate behavior of gold prospectors that triggered the outbreak of war. Coincident with the treaty, gold was being discovered all over eastern Washington and in what eventually became British Columbia. Prospectors leaving the played-out California goldfields and the Australian gold digs trickled and then swarmed into the Northwest to look around, absolutely contrary to the not-yet-ratified Yakima Treaty of 1855. Traditionally a rough, independent lot, the miners asked no favors of anyone and gave no quarter, either. They banded together into small groups and walked across Indian lands en route to their prospect holes.

Indian women suffered at the hands of the miners, whose brutalities enraged the natives. To its credit, the Army tried to contain the flood of often-lawless prospectors, but in the arid and trackless eastern Washington plains, deserts, and complicated foothills, it was impossible to control them all.

The situation escalated. Colonel E. J. Steptoe ventured north to confront the Indians and was soundly defeated in a battle near Spokane in May 1858. All of eastern Washington became a powder keg. There were random shootings of Indians and incidents between squatters, legitimate ranchers, and Indians bent on revenge. In a June 1858 engagement that cost Quiltenenock his life, he and Quetalican attacked a party of seventy-six California miners who had come from what is now Blewett Pass and intended to turn north along the Columbia. A lively battle took place at the site of the present-day city of Wenatchee. Skamow, the Wenatchi chief, came to the miners' assistance, since he regarded his special paper from Wright as a sort of alliance. As soon as they could disengage from the battle, the miners retreated toward The Dalles, the area from which they had come.

With Quiltenenock's death, Quetalican became the acknowledged leader of the Columbia band. He began to speak on behalf of the Wenatchis, too, after he adopted his dead father's name of Half-Sun. To the whites he was known simply as Moses, the name given to him at the mission school he had attended in Lapwai, Idaho.

Back at the Vancouver barracks of the U.S. Army, Department of the Columbia, headquarters, now under General Newman F. Clarke's leadership, a major offensive was planned to punish the Indians who had defeated Steptoe and also to locate those who had attacked the miners. With a force of 570 men, Wright headed for Coeur d'Alene, meeting and defeating the hostile Indians at Four Lakes and Spokane Plains. Meanwhile, troops under Major Robert S. Garnett headed out as the second "prong" of the attack (although there seems to have been poor communication between Wright and Garnett as to each other's whereabouts). Garnett, Lieutenant George Crook, Captain John W. Frazer (head of the Fort Simcoe post), First Lieutenant James K. McCall, and five other line officers plus 286 men left Fort Simcoe for the Wenatchee River valley, their primary task to search for those who had been involved in the battle with the miners. En route, a small detachment under Second Lieutenant Jesse K. Allen detoured twenty miles up the Yakima River to intercept a small band of Indians said to have been involved. Allen lost his life in the skirmish, and the main party came to the rescue of his detachment. Four Indians in the captured party were shot for having participated in the miners' battle (apparently they were identified by Yakima scouts). Captain Frazer accompanied Allen's body back to Simcoe.

On August 18, Garnett's party descended into the Wenatchee Valley from Lake Cle Elum on the Naneum Trail. The troops camped where the town of Wenatchee lies today. Learning that "guilty" Indians were hiding among friendly Wenatchis, Lieutenant Crook and his Company D, comprising seventy-nine men, were dispatched to travel up the Wenatchee River about sixty miles to where the culprits were said to be living. After a difficult trip along a rain-swollen Wenatchee River through Tumwater Canyon, Crook and his party came to a point near Lake Wenatchee where he encountered a youth herding horses. The youth admitted that some of the suspects were in his village and that they had vowed to ambush Crook. Crook wanted to avoid shedding the blood of the innocent host tribe, and asked the youth to get his father. The father and son agreed that Crook should come to the village the following day under the ruse of buying berries, whereupon the chief would quietly point out the guilty Indians and avoid sacrificing his own people. The plan was carried out, and five natives were accused and shot; some accounts said they were nailed or tied to trees first. One was a medicine man. According to his biographer, Martin F. Schmitt, Crook described the scene as follows:

> I had them all pinioned, and then told them the object of my mission, and that I intended shooting them before I left. I wanted them to make any final preparations they wished, and reasonable time would be given them, etc. etc. They all acknowledged their guilt, but made the excuse that they were forced or persuaded by others, etc. Except the medicine man, who invoked all kinds of curses against us. He called his son to him . . . and made a speech to him in his own tongue.

The son then melted away into the woods. The conversation was later translated; the son had been told to go downriver and ambush the returning troops. Crook's troops took extra precautions thereafter to avoid entrapment.

Crook's party returned safely to Wenatchee. The following day Captain James J. Archer and Second Lieutenant Elisha E. Camp, with sixty men, were detailed to return to the area to pursue another three or four suspects. Accounts of this pursuit vary widely. In one version, which seems to be borne out by Crook's biography and Army records, upon arriving in the upper valley the party found the campsite, but the Indians had fled, so the party returned to camp on August 29, abandoning the search. Crook's biography asserts that Garnett, Crook, and the entire party went on north, not west, and sent a note to Fort Simcoe on September 7.

According to another account, the troops were under Captain Frazer, not Archer and Camp. Accompanied by Yakima guides and probable accusers, the pursuers traveled back into the upper Wenatchee Valley, then up the Chiwawa to the high country of Raging Creek, chasing a group of Indians led by a native named Quolasken. But the group escaped from Frazer by building a makeshift bridge over a twenty-foot-wide chasm to permit their people and horses to cross, and then destroying it behind them.

Native historians have a different account. They say that from Raging Creek, Frazer or some of his men veered south across a ridge into the White River drainage, finding there an extended family of Indians, ten tepees in all, who were picking berries and fishing. Believing them to be the group that had escaped, the soldiers murdered everyone in the camp and burned the tepees. One of the two surviving witnesses was William Harmelt, then a lad tending horses nearby and later the father of the last

The last Wenatchi chief, John Harmelt (Photo: North Central Washington Museum, Wenatchee, WA)

Wenatchi chief, John Harmelt. The young Harmelt fled to a camp of relatives near today's Cashmere and related the horrible tale. No doubt fearing further bloodshed, the Indians kept the matter to themselves.

On the other hand, Byron Dickinson, a lifelong resident of the upper valley, says that in about 1918, area residents Lester Brown and George

Schugart found two small cannons, muzzle down, standing against a fir tree at the edge of Raging Creek, but later they were unable to find them again. Dickinson also says that there is no chasm in the area as narrow as twenty feet and that, without ropes and pitons, it would have been impossible for the soldiers to go directly from Raging Creek to White River, as is alleged in the Indians' account. One would have to detour northwest and go through the Twin Lakes Creek drainage.

Still another version is related by Edson Dow, a retired U.S. Forest Service (USFS) ranger, in his 1963 book *Passes to the North*. He asserts that the pursued Indians split up, with some going up the Chiwawa and some fleeing north up Raging Creek: "According to local tradition, both Indians and whites lost their lives as a result of this conflict up Raging Creek. [Yet] Army reports on file show no soldiers reported missing. A common grave area has been recently discovered."

In the early 1900s, homesteader Lawrence Dickinson found scattered human bones in a particular area of the White River valley. No one could enlighten him as to the identities of the dead. In 1974, a USFS historian speculated that the bones' location might verify the account of the massacre. USFS archaeologists said that the apparent age of the bones was consistent with the whispered accounts of the atrocity, although the damage to the fragile remains from a 1915 forest fire in the area, coupled with the sheer age of the bones, made an accurate assessment difficult, if not impossible.

The truth about the incident may be a composite of these various versions. Proponents of the highly diverse stories hold strong opinions, and the author is unable to sort out the differences in the accounts.

After Wright's army defeated the Indians at Four Lakes and Spokane Plains, the units returned to Fort Simcoe, The Dalles, and Walla Walla. Except for isolated incidents, the Indian wars ceased.

In the Leavenworth area, Indian groups resumed their annual fishing at Wenatshapam, berrying and hunting around Lake Wenatchee, and wintering in more permanent homes near the town of Mission (which was later renamed Cashmere). At Mission, the Jesuits had converted many Wenatchis. Father L. Napoleon St. Onge visited the Wenatchis around 1867, while he was working among the Yakimas. Father Urban Grassi came to the Wenatshapam fishery in 1873 to reacquaint the Indians with Catholicism, only to find their chief, Patoi, teaching a religious creed that blended old native beliefs with Father Grassi's convictions. Working with the chief, who was a bit belligerent about whose authority his people should respect, the priest renewed his relationship with the native people, eventually establishing a small mission building in 1874 near today's Cashmere, naming it St. Francis Xavier. The settlers moving into the Wenatchee country lived peaceably with the Indians, but only a handful of white settlers lived upstream on the Wenatchee River.

Meanwhile, the Indian leader known to whites as Moses had become wise to the ways of white politicians and had learned to play their game masterfully. Because Moses was colorful and outspoken, whites viewed him as a spokesman for the bands along the Columbia, including the Wenatchis. But when he refused to move to the Yakima Reservation with his people in the late 1870s and the Nez Percé War erupted, ending with Nez Percé leader Chief Joseph's famous flight through the Bitterroot Mountains, whites feared that Moses might be fomenting dissent among the peaceful bands for whom he purportedly spoke.

In truth, Moses wanted his own reservation. Although his band had roamed throughout an area of over a hundred square miles, his homeland was around Moses Coulee, east of the Columbia, in today's Douglas County. Unable to obtain this land officially, Moses took his case to Washington, D.C. officials, with whom he seemed perfectly at ease. As a result, in 1879, he secured a proposal for a Columbia Reservation extending from Lake Chelan northward to the international border and from the North Cascades east to the Okanogan River.

After Moses had returned home, the government officials asked for a conference to discuss the matter, hoping other mid-Columbians would move to Moses's reservation. Moses, Chief William Harmelt of the Wenatchis, and other affected chiefs came to Wenatchee Flats in 1879 to confer. On behalf of the government, no less than the territorial governor, Elisha P. Ferry, and General O. O. Howard were among the attendees. It was a colorful occasion, graphically described in *Century Magazine* by Lieutenant C. E. S. Wood:

> The first general meeting was at the mouth of the Wenatchee, in the heart of the ruggedest Alps of America. The great Columbia tore through the mountain pass in a grand sweep, tossing and foaming. This bend of the river inclosed a level plain some mile or so broad. . . . We arrived first and went into camp. The pack-mules luxuriated in good rolls in the sand, the canvas village arose, and very soon bacon and coffee led us to supper by the nose. Next morning our friends began to arrive. The news of our presence flew in that way so mysterious even to those who know the Indian's tireless night-and-day riding and system of signaling. Hour after hour the Indians arrived, singly, by families, bands and almost by tribes, trooping in with herds and loaded pack-animals, men, women, and children—for they brought their homes with them. The tepees of buffalo-skin were put up, the smoke of many camp-fires arose, and the hill-sides became dotted with grazing ponies.

The Wenatchis, however, did not want to move to this new place, nor did many of Moses's own people. (Later, in 1883, Moses would sell the reservation back to the government and retire to the Colville Federated Tribes land.) Chief Skamow reiterated the now-ratified Yakima Treaty's promised grant to the Wenatchis of the township-sized, six-square-mile Wenatshapam fishery reservation. The conference dissolved, and the Indians retired to their favorite pastime, horse racing. Wood wrote, "There were on this ground the best horses of the whole Northwest, belonging to rival tribes that had been renowned for horses from the time of Lewis and Clark. There were races almost every hour."

Since the federal land surveys did not include the fisheries (despite its designation in the Yakima Treaty), as the century neared its close, settlers believed the attractive land around Leavenworth and downriver was available, and they attempted to homestead it. When the Great Northern Railroad surveys were completed through Stevens Pass, beginning in 1889 (see Chapter 4), the projected rail line naturally ran through the fishery reservation. About the same time, ranchers downstream laid out various irrigation projects, one of which was an irrigation canal to provide water from the Leavenworth area to the fertile valley lands near Wenatchee. The Wenatchi Indians began to protest.

Around this time a wanderer, Francis Streamer, was traveling through the country, dwelling for lengthy periods with various Indian tribes of eastern Washington. Increasingly he championed the Indians' causes and wrote voluminously to government officials; increasingly, too, he became entirely deranged. Entries in his carefully kept diary started out sensibly enough, but then went into endless tirades about history, government, social issues, and Streamer's apparent belief that he was destined to be a key figure on the world stage. He wrote well, if in flowery language, about the Leavenworth scenery:

> My position is on a rock boulder, high up on the western side of the rim of the mountain. Through and around the base of which—serpentine and splash the ever-green waters of the Wenatchee river—about twenty-five miles from its mouth—by its course from the northwest and within a mile of its junction of Nysickle and Peshastin rivers. I have a commanding view of the west range of mountains gorged and graven in granite gray boulders of beautiful texture and wealth of vesture. The falls are below me and foam and roam the river's green in sheaths and sheen—poetically serene. On the other side of the Falls is my old Indian friend Dominiqe [sic] and his family, spearing and drying salmon for their winter's food. I arrived yesterday—July 17, 1890.

Proceeding from such simple narration, his prose went on to reflect increasing irrationality:

Generations to come will, therefore, appreciate these sacred lands, and great will be the palatial residences of scholars, philosophers, builders, some writers of instruction in these Wenatchee Mountains, long years after this writer will have been gathered unto his aboriginal fathers; and this Book of Life—published and illustrated in all parts of the Great and Good Governments of this Redeemed Land—for upon these lands was it first written by Francis Marion Streamer—the true message writer—who is now known to all nations for his defense of the poor of all races, sects.

Nevertheless, in response to his writings to General O. O. Howard, then back East, the fishery matter was addressed. Surveyor George W. Gordon had investigated the matter in early 1889, listening to the opinions of several local people on where the fishery's six square miles were centered, concluding that the site was about six miles from the junction of the Icicle and Wenatchee rivers, down to the town of Mission. He recommended that the matter be resolved before there was trouble.

On September 8, 1892, Indian agent Joe Lynch came from Yakima (the Wenatchis were still allied with the Yakimas in the eyes of the government) to determine exactly where the fishery was. Instead of construing the boundaries of the fishery to be the forks of the river embracing the Icicle and Wenatchee, as the Indians believed, Lynch conveniently chose the Wenatchee-Chiwawa forks far upriver and ordered that area to be surveyed officially.

In July 1893, Commissioner of Indian Affairs D. M. Browning suggested in an open letter to Wenatchee Valley's white settlers that they write to President Benjamin Harrison asking him to sell the Wenatshapam fishery reservation. Upon receipt of such letters, the Office of Indian Affairs moved to buy the land, planning to offer the Indians $10,000 for the fishery.

Since the Wenatchis were presumed to be bound by the Yakima Treaty of 1855, the meeting was held at the Yakima Indian Agency on December 18 and 19, 1893, 100 miles from the Wenatchis' valley. Only three Wenatchi leaders made it through the bitterly cold weather and deep snow. Although they spoke eloquently against the proposal, calling to mind the grant they had received almost forty years earlier, they tentatively agreed to consider a proposal granting eighty acres each to the approximately 125 Wenatchis in the area, plus $10,000 for the fishery.

The three Wenatchi leaders went home to discuss the matter. Without their presence, the Yakima leaders agreed to sell the fishery for $20,000 plus the allotments of land mentioned. The Yakimas were to use the money as they saw fit. In March 1896, the Yakimas used the money to construct an irrigation system that benefited Yakima Reservation people but came nowhere near the Wenatchee Valley. The government allotment of land took years to resolve, so that by the time the lands actually began to be surveyed and allotted under fair and friendly Indian agent William Casson, most of the good lands in the Wenatchee Valley had already been homesteaded by white settlers. In fact, by 1900, there was not enough unclaimed land available for all the tribal members. About eighty families chose to take up their allotments on the Colville Reservation; others stayed on stubbornly in their homelands, mostly around Cashmere, rather than at Leavenworth, the site of the fishery. As the Wenatchis had children and grandchildren, the lands were divided again and again until they were of impractical size for farming.

Two disease epidemics decimated the Wenatchis. Gradually the Wenatchi descendants moved away, many to the Colville Reservation. By 1927, it was reported that the only remaining Wenatchis were Kami Sam (Ktienecht) and his sister Clotilda Judge (Teesahkt), Indian Felix (Popspaan), Johnnie Baker, and Chief John Harmelt and his wife, Ellen (Quihonmeet).

In 1931, a Cashmere attorney spearheaded a renewed effort to get fair reimbursement for the Wenatchis, calling attention to their plight with a public-relations stunt—a grand powwow with an encampment, games, and other colorful events that attracted both Indian and white visitors.

Chief John Harmelt and his wife did not live to see the settlement of the matter; they were killed in a house fire on July 4, 1937. It was not until July 29, 1963, that the Wenatchi descendants were finally reimbursed retroactively for the lands in a joint decision involving several other tribes and other unfair land transactions. The Yakimas and the Colville Confederated Tribes (with whom most of the Wenatchis were living by then) received a $4 million settlement for the lands, based on the 1859 value of the land: 50 cents an acre.

3. EARLY WHITE SETTLERS

The first white settlement at the eastern end of Stevens Pass was located where the town of Cashmere stands today. Established by Jesuit Father Respari in 1863, it was a log-cabin mission on Mission Creek. (A replica is exhibited at the Willis Carey Museum Pioneer Village at Cashmere.) Later, Father Urban Grassi and his followers replaced the small building with a larger one that included a school.

Until decades later, when the road through Stevens Pass was carved out, the chief access route from south and west was through the pass known today as Blewett Pass, an early site of gold prospecting. A man named Ben Ingalls played an important, if indirect, role in drawing people to the area. According to John Hansel, a close friend of Ingalls who settled near Peshastin, Ingalls and a party of fifty men entered the Wenatchee Valley in the spring of 1861, looking for a gold ledge Ingalls had seen on an earlier trip. West of what is now Cashmere, Ingalls led the party along a sandstone bluff beside the Wenatchee River. He walked under a willow tree and, when a limb caught on his pick, he called to Jack Knot, the man behind him, to warn Knot of the limb. Just then the willow disengaged and whipped back to catch in the hammer of Knot's loaded gun, discharging it into Ingalls's back. Ingalls lived for an agonizing two nights and a day, injured in his spine and stomach. Before dying, he told Hansel the approximate location of the gold prospect—somewhere on the creek that would later be known as Ingalls

Creek—but neither Hansel nor anyone else ever found the deposit. Some speculate that the earthquake of 1872 rearranged the terrain around Table Mountain, Red Hill, and Tip-top Peak, to which Ingalls had directed his friend. Others speculate that the color Ingalls had seen was in fact near Clark and Marion lakes, the Enchantment Lakes, or Lake Ingalls. While the gold *ledge* Ingalls described was never found, gold was discovered in 1873 along Ingalls Creek and, indeed, all over the Blewett and Ingalls areas—leading to an influx of miners, prospectors, and the more staid homesteaders.

The miners and Hudson's Bay trappers merely passed through the Wenatchee Valley, but Alexander Brender was the first permanent settler, in 1881, homesteading in Brender Canyon on a piece of land now on Pioneer Avenue in downtown Cashmere. In 1882, D. S. Farrar planted the valley's first orchard with trees he had brought with him from Yakima; and in 1887, Oliver McManus homesteaded 322 acres in Brender Canyon. With a $25 stake, Al Moorehouse started a general store in 1888, and the post office of the town, then called Mission, opened in 1889. It was off and running as a settlement, although it did not get its present-day name until after it was incorporated in 1904. At

The town of Cashmere began as a log-cabin mission established on Mission Creek in 1863. (Photo: Don Seabrook, The Wenatchee World)

that time there were other Washington towns called Mission, causing confusion for the mail service. Local judge James Chase was enchanted by the poetry of Sir Thomas Moore and his "Vale of Kashmir." With creative misspelling, he chose the name Cashmere for the village around 1906.

Upriver, two bachelors, John Emig and Nicholas Kinscherf, homesteaded side by side near the site of present-day Leavenworth. George Briskey came from Klickitat County in 1885 to homestead at Icicle Flats, he and his wife becoming the first residents of Icicle. He was joined by his extended family and that of F. D. Estes four years later. The Briskey family's first winter home was a one-room cabin with pole bunks and flour sacks stuffed with hay for mattresses. The David C. Wilson family lived in the Icicle/Leavenworth area from 1890 to 1905. Around 1891, F. A. Losekamp established a ten-by-ten-foot store on the south bank of the Wenatchee River at Icicle, becoming its first postmaster, too. Other early homesteaders included Mary Ralston, who taught the first school, founded in 1893; beekeeper Ralph Fisher; and farmer Albert Walker. Charles Cromwell came in 1892 to raise fruit and alfalfa; he moved to the Chumstick Valley in 1895.

The pace quickened as the Great Northern Railroad (GNR) tracks stretched ever westward toward Stevens Pass. By March 1892, the grading crews were close to Icicle. The GNR bought some property—a mile long and 400 feet on either side of its tracks—to accommodate its division facilities. Obligingly, merchants of the town of Icicle disbanded and moved to the site of present-day Leavenworth.

Wendell E. Stevens established the first sawmill up Mission Creek in 1889, followed by the Schmitten Lumber Company in 1902. C. H. Wright started a mill at Dryden, between Cashmere and Leavenworth. Miners in Blewett Pass added to the area's growing economy.

Tumbling out of the Cascades through Tumwater Canyon, the Wenatchee River left no room for westerly development. To the north and northwest, though, a big bulge of relatively flat land laced with ridges and forests attracted early homesteaders to Lake Wenatchee and the Chumstick and Beaver Creek valleys.

The earliest homesteaders of the settlement called Beaver Valley (later renamed Plain), around 1891, were E. D. (Charles) Schugart; his wife, Priscilla (she died young, and Schugart later remarried); and a trapper named John Matthews, who had "squatter's rights" on 160 acres. Then came W. W. Burgess in 1893, the head of a colorful family still prominent in the valley. Originally from Iowa, W. W. first tramped through western Washington and then Okanogan County toward the

Canadian border before he found and fell in love with Beaver Valley. After buying Matthews's quarter-section and rough log cabin, W. W. went to Orcas Island to claim his bride, Elizabeth. The two came to Leavenworth in July 1895 for provisions and a wagon and two horses, and then started over a rough trail to Beaver Valley. Descendants say that when the couple came over Beaver Hill and W. W. stopped to point out his log cabin, which was sitting in the center of a dense forest, his bride cried. Their only close neighbors were the Schugarts; otherwise the tall mountains, wild animals, and trees were the Burgesses' sole companions. Leavenworth was fifteen miles away over a rough trail. After comforting his wife, W. W. cut down a tree and tied it to the rear of their wagon to slow their descent into the valley. So began their married life.

Despite her original dismay, Elizabeth pitched in industriously to help W. W. clear the valley, uncovering fertile land that produced grass to feed livestock. W. W. was a natural engineer, designing and fashioning such devices as a stump puller and an all-wooden threshing machine, powered by a home-designed waterwheel, to thresh the wheat grown as a cash crop on the newly cleared land. During the dry summer, he irrigated crops from Beaver Creek by simple flooding techniques. When the creek failed to accumulate sufficient water for irrigation, W. W. diverted another stream at the top of Entiat Ridge into Beaver Creek. About 1910–11, the Chiwawa Irrigation Ditch was constructed to provide an orderly irrigation source.

W. W. built a small sawmill to create lumber for his own buildings and those of new homesteaders moving into the cleared valley. His four brawny sons each had a special task. W. O., also known as Bill, brought logs to the mill carriage, which moved them past the saw to be cut into lumber of varying sizes. Son Bahn cut the bark-covered slabs into suitable sizes for firewood. Jack was the fireman engineer for the power-driven machinery of the mill, such as the edger and planer; later, Melvin took over Jack's duties. The mill operated until 1928. Son W. O. then went to the bank, borrowed $100 to buy a team of horses, and logged independently; not until 1938 did he use a tractor.

"Beaver Valley" exceeded the length limit for postal addresses at the time, so the regional postmaster seized upon the name "Plain," the last choice on a twenty-name list given him by locals. In 1910 a religious group, the Dunkards, established a colony nearby.

The handful of pioneers around Plain lived largely off the land; birds, deer, bear, fish, and berries were abundant. One day, while stalking what he thought was a herd of deer, W. W. found a pack of large, gray timber wolves instead; he hastily retreated to safety. There were cougars, too, but they fed mostly on deer and small animals; on rare occasions, the upper Wenatchee Valley pioneers were horrified to find the tracks of cougars that had followed them as potential quarry.

Gypsies sometimes passed through Plain, and Indians came through en route to the Chiwawa ridges or Lake Wenatchee, prime huckleberry grounds. The Indians dried the berries or pounded them into meat to make flavorful pemmican. In the high mountains the Indians also obtained pipestone, a soft stone that could be carved into art works or tobacco pipes. Alpha Burgess Buntain, W. W.'s daughter, wrote in her memoir that a frequent passerby, a woman with the Indian name of Mishee Twie but called Molly, became her special friend:

> One year Molly brought her huckleberries to our house and got permission to dry them on our attic floor. She and I put papers on the floor and spread the berries out on the papers to dry. Molly delegated me to turn them as they dried, and came back later to take them home with her. She gave me an old, badly worn, red blanket for my work. I didn't care—I treasured the old thing for a long time.

One interesting business venture in Plain was David Baker's Fox Farm. Financed by a group of Wenatchee businessmen, the farm raised silver and blue foxes for their fur. The enterprise thrived for some time, until the fur market declined. The foxes were fed horse meat. Buntain recalled attending a bridal shower given by the young men from the farm. The main dish for dinner was a delicious chili, but she gulped a bit after she discovered it too had been made with horse meat.

Ten miles from the settlement around Plain was Lake Wenatchee, hub for a few more homesteaders. The earliest were Oliver and Sally Bates, fresh from the Yukon gold rush, who hoped to cash in on the building of the GNR. They acquired a large tract of land and built the Lakeview Lodge, a small hotel at the northwest end of the lake. Several early surveyors did favor a route up the Little Wenatchee River, but the Bateses lost out when the tracks went up Nason Creek instead. A latter-day critic said the lodge was "right out of an Alfred Hitchcock movie," but it satisfied the earliest wanderers in the area—chiefly those searching for gold, new freight trails, or railroad routes to Puget Sound.

The Bateses sold their hotel in about 1922 to William A. "Cougar Bill" Smith, who renamed it Cougar Inn (the name it still bears today). One day Cougar Bill walked out the back door to go fishing with a friend, never to be seen again. Since then, his ghost has allegedly haunted the place. Visitors claim to have seen such strange things as levitation of objects and a figure that appears and then quickly becomes invisible. Bill is a good ghost, though, never causing trouble.

Although a relatively modest place, Cougar Inn commands a striking view down the lake and has attracted many famous Washingtonians, from members of the Seattle Seahawks to U.S. Senator Warren Magnuson—despite the fact that, in past winters, guests sometimes have had to crawl out the attic windows after a heavy snowfall. During earlier years, when access to the upper Wenatchee Valley was limited, locals enlivened the winters by throwing potluck wing-dings at the inn.

After the Bateses, the next settlers on Lake Wenatchee were William and Sarah Blankenship, in 1890. Some time after moving to the area, Blankenship built Dirtyface Lodge on the lake for the Lamb-Davis Lumber Company, which used it to entertain visiting businessmen and employees of the company. Unfortunately, the lodge burned down in October 1944.

George Siverly, a trapper working with a man named Johnny Cody (who was said to be a nephew of Buffalo Bill), came into the White River area at about the same time as the Bateses and the Blankenships. Siverly told a reporter that he and Cody trapped marten, lynx, bobcat, and fisher and that on November 19, 1899, they killed three grizzly bears, one a silvertip whose hide he sold for $50.

Before 1900, there was no boat service on Lake Wenatchee. Then came the *Clara D*, a rough-hewn passenger and freight boat. Named for the operator's wife, Clara D. Ott, the boat served lake residents until roads and trails were built (there still is no through road on the south side of the lake). At first, residents brought freight with a team to one side, the *Clara D* took it across the lake, and then a second team picked it up for its destination. People stabled town horses on one side, home horses on the other, and rowed across to feed them.

Around 1906, tourists began to come to Lake Wenatchee. An ad in a 1906 *Wenatchee World* proclaimed that one could ride to Winton on the train, take a stage to the foot of Lake Wenatchee, and then ride the *Clara D* motor launch to Dirtyface Lodge—all on the same day.

As early as the 1920s, city people built summer cabins on the lake. Limited hydroplane races were held at that time, but after a cloud of smog hung over the place from the powerful engines, the locals voted them out. In the 1950s, a passenger boat called the *Miss Cougar* operated, but for a time the only other public boats were day boats rented by Cougar Inn. For decades, the cabin residents were well protected by a legendary deputy sheriff, George Carveth, a tobacco-spitting Old West type with a nightstick and gun on his hip, who considered vandalism a personal affront. He always managed to track down offenders.

In the 1930s and 1940s, another small resort with a half-dozen cabins, the Telma Resort, was operated by Georgia Allen, wife of pioneer Dale Allen, who worked in various capacities for the U.S. Forest Service.

Lake Wenatchee's third pioneer family, which still has descendants living in the area, was George and Lois Brown, whose daughter Marie married Lawrence Dickinson—a member of still another pioneer clan. George Brown established the Fish Lake Resort, in 1914 renamed The Cove, which he eventually turned over to his son-in-law Lawrence to operate. It was only a fishing camp of log cabins with rowboats for rent, but it survived until 1965 and was sold in the 1970s.

Lawrence Dickinson homesteaded the property where a Presbyterian camp called Tall Timber now operates. His previous wife, Charlotte, had died in a fire that destroyed the ranch, but Dickinson rebuilt and became a part of the growing logging industry around the lake. During World War II, Lawrence and Marie Dickinson operated a small sawmill near the lake, the site today of Two Rivers Sand & Gravel Company, an enterprise owned by Lawrence and Marie's son Bruce.

Members of the large Dickinson family also operated a small cabin-rental business, a grocery, and the Crescent Beach Dance Pavilion on Lake Wenatchee, a lively spot that was the site of many events, from annual picnics to wrestling matches.

Exploring a remote shore one day, Lawrence Dickinson was startled to discover a low cabin, about four by eight feet, of very sturdy logs, with a secure door marked HBC (for Hudson's Bay Company) and lined by split cedar—obviously a long-unused fur cache. It was Lawrence Dickinson, too, who—quite by accident—discovered the scattered bones thought to be remnants of the alleged massacre of Wenatchi Indians (see Chapter 2).

In 1957, Pastor Edgar Toeves of Moses Lake and other members of the Wenatchee Presbytery purchased Lawrence Dickinson's original homestead, as well as a neighbor's acreage, log home, and six old cabins, for development as a major Presbyterian camp. Volunteers put a program together, and in 1958 the first church camp was held at Tall Timber, using Army cots and food prepared in the old house's kitchen. Jim Adamson, site manager from 1959 to 1965, says:

> It was a pretty primitive affair, with power from a generator, a 500-gallon water tank with pipes that simply went through the walls [which] broke during freezes (usually in the middle of the night) and rubber couplings that failed. We bought a big diesel generator in 1968 and got the pipes put underground.

In 1968, the Presbytery bought another 120 acres, paying for it by subdividing 40 of the acres for private use and selling 35 to the USFS. Local residents and Presbytery volunteers helped to manicure the ranch and build cabins. Use was expanded to include members of the North Puget Sound Presbytery. Adamson, then a high school instructor, ran a wrestling camp for students on the site for about twenty years, until the camp became too tightly scheduled to continue leasing it. Tall Timber was used as a staging area for fire fighters and smoke jumpers during a major fire outbreak in 1970. Today it is completely scheduled most of the time for church-related retreats and camps, winter and summer.

Back in the 1890s, at the same time that the Wenatchee Valley was being settled, a handful of pioneers were moving into the Chumstick Valley, reaching north from Leavenworth. Marion Cahill, a logger for Lamb-Davis Lumber Company, settled there in 1892, joined by Easton Cromwell in 1893. Another early homesteader, Charles Freytag, opened a small sawmill to process the logs on his own and his neighbors' property. As the pleasant valley was opened up by logging, homesteaders moved in. Prior to 1920, investors laid out the town of Appleton, about ten miles from Leavenworth on the Chumstick. They planted apple trees and touted the climate, pointing out that homesteaders could ride a special small passenger coach into Leavenworth. A few people settled there, but the town never materialized. Today, though, now that buildable land at Leavenworth is at a premium, the Chumstick Valley is increasingly becoming a "bedroom community" for the town.

As logging opened up the valley, sheepmen were given contracts to graze herds up the Chumstick and on into the Little Wenatchee/Cady Pass area. An old-time hiker said that in the 1930s, hiking the Cascade Crest Trail was like walking through a vast, groomed park, because the sheep ate down the underbrush. Of course, overgrazing eventually created new problems.

Snows in the area were formidable. In 1915–16, it snowed early and stayed late. By spring, twelve to fourteen feet of snow still lay on the ground, and the farmers above Lake Wenatchee had run out of hay. Over in Plain, kindly pioneer Charlie Schugart had a barn full of hay; he told the farmers that if they could get their stock to his barn, he would feed the animals until the grass came. The farmers started from Tall Timber Ranch on the White River, shoveling out a passable trail all the way to Plain, about fourteen miles away. All the able-bodied members of the twelve to fourteen families pitched in, working in relays and stopping for the night at whatever ranch was closest, and succeeded in saving their stock.

Residents of Plain shoveled tunnels to their outbuildings. The mailman snowshoed from Leavenworth over twelve feet of snow to bring contact with the outside world; desperate settlers struggled to town for vital groceries. When Robert Nickles of Plain developed appendicitis

Leavenworth was often paralyzed in winter by heavy snowfall. (Photo: Special Collections Division, University of Washington Libraries, neg. 4454)

while the roads were totally impassable, twelve neighbors put him on a stretcher and snowshoed with him all the way to Leavenworth, a nine-hour ordeal. The temperature along the Columbia River was eighteen degrees, and big ice jams formed. Train service was halted repeatedly by avalanches. In Leavenworth, snow blocking the streets was shoveled into fifteen- to twenty-foot piles; for residents, it was like living in a maze. When the snow thawed, the rivers and streams flooded. Ordinarily the Wenatchee River was a relatively manageable waterway; however, rapidly melting snow could send it on a rampage.

Snow fell heavily again in 1948, with at least five feet lying on the flat. When the thaw came, fed by a warm rain, the river turned into a raging torrent, inundating the Icicle Valley and turning eastern Leavenworth into one big lake.

Fickle weather patterns did not deter gold prospectors. They found small gold deposits at Ingalls and Peshastin creeks, south of Leavenworth; traces of gold on the Wenatchee River; and asbestos near Mount Stewart. Between Lake Chelan and Canada, there were countless gold strikes in the 1880s and 1890s. Small wonder, then, that around 1891, prospector J. J. Ross said he had made a strike, mainly copper, along the Phelps Creek–Chiwawa River ridge, where Chinese miners had worked earlier.

Rumors of big strikes were common. USFS retiree John Ware recalls a rumor that two prospectors who came to the Panther/Ibex region for several successive summers in the 1860s had hinted at a rich strike. Then one fall, only one of the partners came out, and he never returned in the spring, so no one had any idea of the find's whereabouts.

A July 26, 1979, *Leavenworth Echo* article told of an early find called the Lost Cabin Mine. A German man appeared at Miller's store (a pioneer business in Wenatchee) with gold, saying that his partner had been killed by a grizzly and that he was returning to Europe. He took others back into the Entiat Mountains to show them where he had found the gold, but en route he fell to his death, and his secret died with him.

Just two miles from Leavenworth, on Hog Back Mountain in Tumwater Canyon, John Sadoske of Idaho claimed to have found a vein of quartz yielding $20,000 to the ton. The whole mountain was filed upon by spring.

Numerous claims were filed on Red Mountain as well—by Lamb-Davis Lumber Company, North Star Mining Company, and others. A colorful prospector, Red Mountain Ole (whose real name was John Smith), roamed the ridge for years, bringing in silver-fox skins that fetched more money than any gold dust.

In 1905, an invitation to bid was distributed for building a twenty-four-mile wagon road to Red Mountain, from a point somewhere between Plain and Lake Wenatchee—a road that proponents said would be extended over the Cascades into Darrington via Buck Creek Pass, and on into Seattle. The state legislature appropriated $4,000 for the job. Unfortunately, no bidder wanted to tackle it.

The area's only truly promising mine was begun in 1905. Chelan Consolidated Copper Company (CCCC) was organized by easterners and capitalized at $12 million to develop about eighty purportedly rich claims on Red Mountain, about fourteen miles from the famous Holden Mines (separated by a steep, glacier-covered ridge).

On August 9, 1906, CCCC proposed building a standard-gauge railroad from the GNR tracks twelve miles west of Leavenworth, down Nason Creek and up the Chiwawa, to its Red Mountain mine. In 1907, officers of the CCCC talked of building a rail line from the mine to Index. Neither line was built. The wagon road to Red Mountain (known as the Chiwawa Road) did get built, however, with construction completed in 1907. It facilitated the freighting of supplies to the fifteen men boring a tunnel at the mine: five men working each of three eight-hour shifts.

A full crew worked at the Trinity Mine, which was operated by the Royal Development Company. (Photo: courtesy Byron Dickinson)

Although newspapers regularly touted the mine as a boon to Leavenworth and the Wenatchee Valley there were few positive results from the Red Mountain digs until 1916, when J. Lonergan and James Naughten bought up some CCCC claims and formed the Royal Development Company to operate the Royal mine. In that heyday of mining-stock investment, many distant investors had been bilked by claims of promising strikes; some unscrupulous miners would even "seed" a hole with actual minerals taken from elsewhere. Therefore, when the Royal Development Company offered stock and investors found that Naughten's brother, a New York Catholic priest, was handling the financing, they felt sure it was an honest enterprise. Furthermore, the proceeds of stocks were invested in Treasury bonds worth $1.8 million. Only the interest was to be used for development of the mine.

The Royal mine's first discoveries were at Phelps Creek, but due to its unfavorable location for a camp and poor access to the ore body, the campsite was moved to the junction of Phelps Creek and the Chiwawa River. The ore body was accessible from either side of that ridge. There were good amounts of chalcopyrite ore as well as bornite. Experts predicted a yield of forty pounds of copper per ton, with traces of gold and silver. The Royal Development Company had sixteen patented claims and eighty-nine unpatented claims.

The mine was at a high elevation, around 2,900 feet. Still, with great hardship, sixty people constructed the facilities between 1923 and 1928. The area had to be logged off, and the logs removed through ditchlike roads that switchbacked down the grade, so that teams hauling the logs would not be overrun. The best logs were sawed by an on-site mill into lumber for the buildings and mine tunnels. A company town called Trinity grew to include four buildings: an office building, a cookhouse that included a cool house insulated by pumice, a bunkhouse, and a shower house next to the creek. Because of heavy snow and rain, the buildings were connected by covered walkways. Managers and administrators lived in four large houses and five smaller ones, with hot water and reasonable amenities. Bachelors lived in smaller cabins with only cold water. Eventually there were forty-five buildings, including a boardinghouse and commissary, a blacksmith shop, an assay office, and more tidy homes for workers, many of whom brought their families to the site.

Meanwhile, tough men drove a tunnel 11,000 feet into Phelps Ridge from the Trinity side. It was thoroughly engineered, with pipes and fans to provide fresh air; totally electrified; and equipped with a trolley to bring personnel and ore cars into the mine. The trolley turned around in the mine to return with the raw ore. Once at the portal, the material

The camp at Trinity Mine was almost a small village with several substantial buildings. (Photo: courtesy Bryon Dickinson)

was sent by conveyor belt to the milling and concentrating plant, where the ball mill reduced the material to the consistency of flour. This material then went to an ore separator that utilized cyanide and arsenic (in the common separating process of the time, this caused the gold, silver, or copper to rise to the top). Rather considerate of the environment for the time, the builders constructed a dike where tailings were to be dumped, in order to prevent the material from reaching the Chiwawa River. (The tunnel is probably still in fine condition, but it is very securely walled off to protect it from unauthorized entry and potential accident.)

Two water diversion systems (on Phelps Creek and James Creek) and a twelve-foot dam (on Phelps Creek) were constructed; they provide power yet today to the Trinity site's caretakers and owners. The system was designed for fire suppression as well as for the provision of hydroelectric power.

During the decade of operation, the road from Plain to the mine, over which all passengers and freight came, was improved. Workers with money burning holes in their pockets trooped down to Leavenworth to spend it each month, adding to the town's already restless mixture of loggers and railroad men. The mine's managers got the bright idea of bringing the booze to Trinity instead, but it proved difficult during the Prohibition years. For one shipment, a man and woman dressed as a priest and nun took a wagonload of liquor through a blockade. Another delivery driver was found dead on the trail one day, having imbibed too much of his product.

At Chikamin Flats, about halfway to the mine from Leavenworth, a log house provided shelter for miners coming and going in bad weather; there was another house at Rock Creek. Winter's extreme snows and cold were a challenge for Trinity's residents. In archived memoirs at the Leavenworth Ranger Station, an unidentified woman, seven months pregnant, described her trip out to Leavenworth, where she would stay until March. She, her eighteen-month-old son, the wife of Trinity's manager, and four men set out during a heavy January snowstorm:

> We rode quite comfortably in a covered stoneboat lined on the inside with old-fashioned three-piece mattresses. They had fastened the man-sled on top, with snowshoes for everyone on the sides, in case of emergency. Along with the baggage piled on top, we must have made quite a sight!

It took all day to cover six miles over the ten-foot snowpack, at times cutting out trees that blocked the trail. After spending the night in the Rock Creek way station, the party covered only four miles the second day to the big log house at Chikamin. The worst part lay ahead: traversing a trail cut across a continuous rockslide (it still exists as a road today), where a misstep might cause one to plunge 500 feet over a precipice. The pregnant woman described the awful day:

> Continuously during the trip the snow would pile up in front of the tractor, making it necessary to back up to the stoneboat and then lunge ahead full speed to get through. Frequently it would simply sink and then they would have to uncouple, dig out and then go on for perhaps an hour. . . . Several times while crossing [the cut] the stoneboat would slip and swing downward causing an indescribably sinking feeling, but that Godsend of a tractor never faltered.

In 1924, four miners were traveling to Trinity with loads of fuse. With the temperature at thirty-eight degrees below zero, the men moved briskly. Fred Ruth, age nineteen, traveled light and broke trail. He soon complained that he could not feel his feet anymore. Ignoring the advice of the older men to stop and get his circulation going, he chose to just move faster. When he reached the way station, he started a fire and put his feet in the oven. Only when his stockings and pants began to burn did he realize that his feet were actually frozen beyond feeling. By the time the other men reached camp, Ruth was in excruciating pain from too-rapid thawing. One man rushed on to Trinity, reaching there at 3:00 A.M. and procured a sled and assistance to bring Ruth back to Leavenworth for treatment. The Leavenworth Forest Ranger Station sent a wagon as far as possible to meet the sled. After forty-six hours of travel, the four men got Ruth to Leavenworth. His legs were saved, but the four men were also suffering from exposure and had to be hospitalized for several days.

Just preparing for mining consumed an enormous amount of both time and money. After more than seven years of construction, the Royal mine started shipping ore in 1929. With full production, trucks began to haul ore to Leavenworth for transport to the Tacoma Smelter by rail. The first carload was shipped on October 20, 1929.

There was every indication of progress. In August 1930, a modern concentrating mill was installed, after the heavy machinery had been transported over the long, primitive road. In mid-September, backer Naughten visited the mine and expressed amazement at the activity. Yet, after fifteen carloads of ore had been sent to the Tacoma Smelter (with satisfactory yields, it is believed), in October 1930 notice came from the eastern financiers to close down immediately. No reason was given, but the closure order was probably related to the stock-market crash and the growing national depression, since the company appeared to be in financial difficulty.

Dismayed miners, all settled with their families at Trinity Mine, rioted but had no recourse, and most had to seek other employment. In September 1931, at least two eastern investors, Waldo Longwell and James G. McLaughlin, a former director, filed a suit against the company for breach of contract. James Naughten, who had been the mine superintendent since the beginning, vehemently declared that the firm was sound and would be able to retire its indebtedness by the following spring with the revenue from ore sales. A devastating battle between management and stockholders dragged on for several years, with Naughten wanting to operate the mine and claiming that the indebtedness was incurred only through advance expenses in servicing several contracts in hand. The mine did operate on a limited basis from 1931 to 1936 under a lease to a Canadian group, employing about fifty men, but it again closed suddenly after one carload of concentrate, an especially high grade from hand-selected ore, had been shipped profitably to the smelter. The failure was blamed partially on the disparity in exchange rates between American and Canadian currency.

The company's directors finally removed James Naughten in October 1938, following a survey of the site by officers. He was succeeded by A. J. Kennedy, but stockholders voted to dissolve the company in 1940. Investors did receive 85 cents per dollar invested. Most of the equipment was sold, and in 1946, the property (buildings and 102 mineral claims) was sold to Jesse Smith for $10,000.

After several owners had come and gone, Two Rivers, Inc., acquired the property in 1979 with the intention of building a fine high-country resort, one that would include snowmobiling and cross-country skiing in winter. The owners were discouraged, however, by the heavy snows (as much as ten feet on the ground from November to June), snowslides that wrecked buildings, and the improbability of being able to keep the road open in winter. Byron Dickinson of Two Rivers, Inc., and friends once took snowmobiles to the mine for the day; it snowed fifty-four inches overnight, and they were stuck at the site for a week.

Giving up the resort idea, Two Rivers, Inc., eventually sold most of the property and buildings in 1990 for use as a private vacation estate. With the exception of the dwellings, office, and power-generating facility, all of the processing structures have succumbed to snow or have been destroyed to prevent accidental injury.

Pete McConnell, a lone but friendly trapper, lived along the Chiwawa Road until the 1940s. Pioneer Ralph Newell remembers that

McConnell's sanitation left something to be desired:

> I came up here with W. O. Burgess, who was his friend. Pete smoked Peerless, a very strong pipe tobacco, and I could hardly breathe. Old Pete baked a cake for us in the morning. I started to dig into the cake and it would hardly come apart, it was so full of dog hair. My son Bill, who was with us, said, "Wow, it's full of salt instead of sugar." Well, he eventually moved to a Leavenworth nursing home. I suspect his biggest problem was from the Peerless!

McConnell was buried in June 1948 at a small cemetery near Plain on the Burgess property. Two of his fellow prospectors and trappers, Red Mountain Ole and Blue Mountain Ole, are buried along the Chiwawa River.

Amplifying stories of the past presence of the Hudson's Bay Company in the area was the report by a prospector who found an adit (a passage from a mine to the surface) somewhere near McConnell's cabin site, crawled in, and found it was indeed an old mine. Near the site was a board with the words "Hudson's Bay Company, March [date unreadable], L. Swyne, foreman." A pack trail, a small ore dump, and a collapsing footbridge across the stream left no further clues as to the prospector's identity.

Also near McConnell's cabin site, Ralph Newell recounts, a sheepherder employed by Paul Lauzier, Sr., to monitor sheep in the Napeequa range carved a face on a tree with "M L 1914" below. The tree was felled by a logger, who carefully severed the portion of wood with the face and inscription and brought it to the Lake Wenatchee Ranger Station, where it can be seen today.

THE RAILROAD

4. THE SEARCH
FOR STEVENS PASS

By 1881, the Indians' worst fears had been realized. The iron rails of the Northern Pacific Railway were completed to join Spokane with the Columbia River's new towns and cities, looping through eastern Washington's traditional Indian lands. There was no stopping the influx of white settlers.

The North Cascades stood as a formidable barrier to east-west commerce farther north. James J. Hill, the head of the Minnesota-based Great Northern Railroad, had his eye on the increasing wheat production in eastern Washington and a keen interest in the Orient trade. To compete with the Northern Pacific for those markets, the GNR needed to find some way to put its rails through from Spokane to a Puget Sound port that provided the shortest access time for freighters to and from the North Pacific. Survey parties tramped through the mountains from the Canadian border to Snoqualmie Pass, but Stevens Pass still lay hidden.

Meanwhile, U.S. government officials discussed building a military road from Fort Steilacoom on lower Puget Sound to Bellingham at the north. At the point where the projected road crossed the Snohomish River, a development group led by Steilacoom speculator E. C. Ferguson filed land claims through agents for a new town of Snohomish City. In 1858–59, gold fever broke out, from the Cascades near Bellingham all the way east to what is today northeastern Washington. Seizing the opportunity to supply the prospectors rather than look for gold himself,

Ferguson and others negotiated with engineer E. F. Cady to search for a pass over the Cascades. Since Port Townsend, Port Gamble, and Port Ludlow merchants hoped to reap benefits from ship traffic inbound for the new goldfields, they contributed to the search.

In the fall of 1859, Cady and a man named Parsons bushwhacked their way up the north fork of the Skykomish River to discover Cady Pass, between today's Henry M. Jackson Wilderness and Glacier Peak Wilderness. The lateness of the season then caused them to turn back.

The following spring, Cady (under Ferguson's direction) hired a crew to hack out a crude trail, which terminated about five miles short of the pass when funds ran out. To demonstrate the practicability of the projected trail, Cady and Ferguson, with four horses, traveled over Cady Pass, down Cady Creek to its junction with the Little Wenatchee River, and on to the Columbia River. They continued to northeastern Washington, only to return with the news that the reportedly rich goldfields

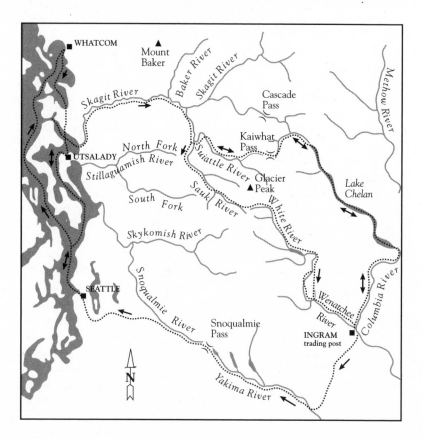

were unimportant finds. They retreated to Snohomish City and abandoned the trail-building venture. Nonetheless, the route Cady pioneered influenced almost all future explorations.

The Northern Pacific's first official exploration of the North Cascades took place in 1867 under General James G. Hilton. The effort included J. S. Hurd and W. C. H. Carlton. Carlton went to the headwaters of the Skykomish River, and another man went to the Skagit. Neither favored any route north of Snoqualmie Pass.

Three years passed before another organized attempt at conquering the North Cascades was made, this time by D. C. Linsley, who was under orders from Edwin H. Johnson, chief engineer of the Northern Pacific, to probe any possible route around forty-eight degrees latitude. Linsley started from Whatcom (today's Bellingham) on May 25, 1870, and traveled by canoe up the Skagit River into the Sauk River. Linsley's plan was to explore passes toward Lake Chelan, which meant veering into the Suiattle River. The Indian canoeists and guides revolted at this idea, pointing out the extreme hardships of the route. After a day's negotiation, the Indians agreed to accept a pay raise, and went on. On June 5, the party could go no farther by canoe and continued by foot, packing basic supplies. They left the Suiattle and turned up what they called Kaiwhat Creek, probably today's Sulphur Creek. In a diary entry published in *Northwest Discovery*, Linsley described the magnificent scenes that appeared before him:

> From the north bank of this creek the snow peaks [Downey Mountain, Spire Point, Dome Peak] rise almost perpendicularly. Any number of little rivulets creep out from under the enormous snow banks and tumble down the rocky sides of the mountains. I noticed one which I estimated falls a thousand feet in a nearly perpendicular descent. . . . The cedar particularly is most remarkable. I think on some acres 20 trees might be cut that would square 15 in. for 50 ft. and be perfectly straight. The fir timber is als[o] very fine, thick and thrifty but not so large as I have seen lower down.

Linsley's party had easy going up the Kaiwhat for a while, but on June 7, as they followed a very faint, seldom-used trail, passage became rugged. Linsley wrote:

> Although the summit of the pass is distant from our camp but about one and one-half miles and we had no luggage, yet so steep and difficult was the ascent that with the utmost diligence we did not reach the summit until half past seven a.m. [they left at 4:15 A.M.]. . . . The elevation of the Pass is 6,135 ft. above tide.

Linsley reported that the railroad could only pass through the area by a tunnel a mile or a mile and a half long, noting that the mountains were of granite.

After a tough twenty-five-mile return trip to the river, the party again took to the river, heading back to the Sauk. The rain-swollen Suiattle was swift and full of rapids. While Linsley was frightened by the river's turbulence, he was able to admire the skill of his crew:

> Just ahead a line of white and tossing foam stretches entirely across the stream from bank to bank. . . . To enter that line of barring breakers seems the wildest madness. . . . [The Indians'] black eyes, fairly glistening with excitement, are riveted on the wild whirls into which we are rushing. But we are close upon the foremost breaker. A volley of gutterals breaks forth from the chief in the stern and is answered by similar sounds from each of the crew. The poles are dropped to the bottom and by an instantaneous and powerful jerk the canoe's course is changed a trifle, so that it clears by a hand's breadth the first rock we meet. . . . Your eye catches glimpses of the rocks as you fly by . . . you literally bail for life. A moment more and the triumphant shout of the Indians rises above the roar of the water and announces that you are for the moment safe.

After struggling up the Sauk and waiting for advance parties bringing supplies to the summit, Linsley set out from his camp and reached the summit on June 30, somewhat north of Cady Pass. Linsley described this moment:

> We reach the head of the valley, which has an elevation of about 3700 ft. above tide. . . . Turning abruptly to the Left, we ascend a very steep ridge some 1300 ft high and stand upon the summit of the pass, 5042 ft. above the sea [Indian Pass]. . . . The Pass is about forty to fifty rods wide and half a mile long . . . it is bounded on both sides by Peaks [Kodak Peak and Indian Head Peak] 1500 to 3000 ft. higher than the Pass itself.

Although the Indians insisted there was no other practical pass, guide John Tennant and Linsley climbed Indian Head Peak and discovered a pass on the north side of the peak (now known as Linsley Pass) that was a shorter distance across—5,378 feet—than Indian Pass. Linsley decided that this would be a practical place for a tunnel about one and a half miles long. He declared that he could see no better pass in either direction from the peak.

Linsley and his party made their way down the eastern slope about five miles to where their horses were waiting, and continued on to the Columbia River. After a trip up Lake Chelan to explore a possible connection to Kaiwhat Creek, Linsley returned to Seattle via Snoqualmie Pass. When he left the Chelan area, his party had nothing left but bacon and flour, and the cooking utensils consisted of a frying pan, a knife and fork, and a tin cup.

Linsley reported that the route from the mouth of the Skagit River over Linsley Pass and on to Spokane would cost $13 million, or $39,000 per mile; the Chelan route, $16 million. In July 1872, under the direction of Thomas B. Morris, engineer for the Northern Pacific, field surveyors H. S. Ward and J. T. Sheets ran lines over what was essentially Linsley's route. They suffered great hardship. When Morris came from the Skagit Valley to locate the two surveyors, he found Sheets half-starved with only unleavened bread to eat. Other engineers in the area doing location work included D. K. Birnie, J. Y. Buchanan, L. A. Habersham, Philip G. Eastwick, J. R. Maxwell, and James T. McFabe. After reviewing all available survey reports, V. G. Bogue, engineer of the Cascade Division surveys, concluded on April 25, 1882:

> . . . there is no place to cross the mountains north of Snoqualmie Pass where a great deal of money would not be necessary both in first cost of construction and in subsequent operation. . . . It is certain that the snowfall is greater on northern portions of the range than between the Snoqualmie and Natchess [sic] Passes.

The Northern Pacific's route went through Stampede Pass in 1887. Meanwhile, James J. Hill continued his probing of the more northerly passes as part of his effort to extend the GNR's rails ever westward from Minnesota through construction and mergers. Even as he searched for a pass through the Rocky Mountains, he was considering the formidable Cascades, which though not as high were exceedingly steep. Albro Martin, Hill's biographer, wrote of the magnate: "All his hopes were pinned on a scrawny, dundreary-whiskered, tobacco-stained, and foul-mouthed little man, an Army engineer, 'poor old Major Rogers,' as Hill called him."

In 1887 that engineer, Albert Bowman Rogers, probed the North Cascades. In earlier years, Rogers had located the pass through the Selkirk Mountains for the Canadian Pacific Railway and had had other successes as well. He started from Missoula, Montana, with two men, and by June 17, 1887, he was in Waterville to begin his serious search of the Cascades. On July 1 at Wenatchee, he wrote in his diary, "No flour, oatmeal to be had at Wenatchee. Can get 15 lbs bacon at Lower Ferry and 20 lbs beans at Freer and Miller's—nothing else—got track of 2 men at Mission Creek who may have bacon and beans."

Having gathered eighteen pounds of beans (but no bacon) at Mission Creek, the men explored Lake Chelan's upper reaches first: the Railroad Creek drainage and part of the Stehekin River. By late July Rogers was back at Miller and Freer's store for supplies. Starting up the Wenatchee River, he commented on July 28 that the mosquitoes and gnats were driving the horses wild. The following day he watched the Indians fishing at the mouth of the Icicle River and visited with an Indian called Salt Chuck. Taking the advice of the Indians, he abandoned any plans to struggle up the Tumwater Canyon and veered off through the Chumstick Valley toward Lake Wenatchee. On August 2, 1887, he climbed Dirtyface Peak to reconnoiter but found that the valley curved too much and that poor visibility from forest fires prevented clear views.

Rogers and his men took largely the same course up the Little Wenatchee River valley as their predecessors had. Indeed, Rogers mentioned in his diary that he saw bits of blazed trails, even though he made his own way to the divide near Ward's Pass, then walked north along the summit to look down Indian Creek.

Turning back on August 11, Rogers passed Cady Pass and descended the Little Wenatchee to Lake Creek for some rest. Four days later his party went uphill again along Lake Creek, where they met three men from Snohomish City who had come over Cady's trail.

With tenacity and a tolerance for living on meager food and enduring hardship, Rogers continued to consider the White River and then Rainy Creek. Here he was only five miles from what would later be known as Stevens Pass, but that pass eluded him.

Rogers quit at this point, stating in his diary that all the maps he had seen were "fearfully incorrect and mislead one." While the other men returned east, Rogers and one companion started for Snohomish over the Cady Trail, existing in constantly wet clothing and blankets. They were down to one pound of bacon and a mere three inches of flour when they struck a logging camp forty miles west of the summit.

Fortified by a few good meals at the camp, their tattered clothes and blankets dry at last, Rogers and companion reached Seattle by foot, canoe, and steamer on September 6, reporting by letter to his employer, James J. Hill. For the balance of September, Rogers explored the west side of the Cascades, following Linsley's route up the Skagit and Sauk. In his final report to Hill, Rogers wrote that, of all the ground he had covered, he favored the Skykomish–Cady Pass route.

It was left to the legendary surveyor John Frank Stevens, for whom Stevens Pass is rightfully named, to intuitively find the pass. Stevens had earlier made history by discovering Marias Pass, a route through the Rocky Mountains, in 1889. After working for the GNR, he would go on to engineer the Panama Canal.

In 1890, the GNR gave him the task of searching once more for a pass through the Cascades, even as the company continued to extend its rails westward. Like the other explorers, he first examined the mountains above Lake Chelan, for there had always been a difficult, faint, but passable Indian trail above the lake over Cascade Pass. Stevens commented in *An Engineer's Recollections*:

I examined every creek which debouched from the Cascade Mountains eastward into Lake Chelan, but found nothing encouraging. In any case if there had been, Lake Chelan with its extreme depth of water, two or three miles in width, with its practically vertical bluffs along the west shore, would have rendered any route impracticable.

He also explored the Entiat River and mentally designed a railroad paralleling the Northern Pacific from the Columbia River to Cle Elum and over Snoqualmie Pass:

On one of my cruises up the Wenatchee River I had noted a large creek coming into it from the south, well up into the mountains . . . followed up a short distance to where it turned abruptly, coming from the west. . . . I filed that mental picture away in my head for future investigation.

After struggling northwesterly to explore many of the same creeks as his predecessors, Stevens then followed the summit itself southward all the way to Snoqualmie Pass and back, literally crawling on his hands and knees at times over the sharp ridges. Of course, then, he ran across a defile where the headwaters of a creek fell eastward, and wrote that he was confident that it was the head of Nason Creek, which he had noticed earlier. If so, he had found the shortest route from the Wenatchee waters to Puget Sound.

Stevens returned to headquarters and sent his engineer, C. F. B. Haskell, to follow Nason Creek and confirm his hunch. Haskell blazed a tree at the defile with the words "Stevens Pass." As soon as Haskell reported to him, Stevens left the Seattle area and returned to assess what must be done to work westerly from the summit. He later commented, "It is of course well known that the escarpment of the Cascade mountains is everywhere much more abrupt on its west than on its east side, and on the west side lay the problem in this case."

Stevens realized that he must develop a longer grade than the terrain permitted; in other words, he could not just descend by a direct route. Before he left the area, in midwinter and with heavy snows already choking the area, he went into the mountains and "conceived and sketched out the Martin Creek loop, as it was located and built [the loop performs almost a 180-degree turn in its descent]. Early in the spring I had the loop roughly surveyed and finding it practicable, proceeded at once with preliminaries and location from the summit down."

John F. Stevens continued to serve the GNR in various engineering capacities. Toward the end of his life, he settled at Snohomish. He died there on June 2, 1943, at the age of ninety. His years of work for the GNR are commemorated by a bronze statue of him, which stands at Marias Pass in the Rocky Mountains, as well as by Stevens Pass itself, which bears his name.

John F. Stevens, who discovered Stevens Pass, went on to engineer the Panama Canal. (Photo: Special Collections Division, University of Washington Libraries, neg. 3801)

With the GNR's thirty-year search at an end, engineer C. F. B. Haskell finalized the survey for the railroad. In a collection of Haskell's letters to his wife, edited by Daniel C. Haskell, the letter about the engineer's location of Stevens Pass is missing—alas! The collection does, however, include a memo from Stevens in which he described Haskell's trip:

I immediately sent Mr. Haskell to Wenatchee Lake, and to the creek I have described, with orders to follow it up clear to every one of its heads, and that I was very confident he would land in the gap that I had discovered, and if so, to follow through and he would be on the Skykomish River.

The result of this trip was exactly what I had hoped, and expected. The creek—afterwards named Nason Creek, headed directly to the gap, where Mr. Haskell blazed a large tree and marked it "Stevens Pass". . . . There was no evidence whatever that the pass in question was known to anyone. . . . There were no signs of any trails leading to or from it, within ten miles in either direction. No blazes on trees and no signs of any wanderers' camp or camp fires. Heavily timbered—covered with almost impenetrable brush, and not offering any hope that the mountains contained minerals, the region promised nothing to the prospector, while Indians and Whites crossing the mountains used either the Snoqualmie on the south or the Indian Pass on the north for route of transit.

Haskell's descriptions of surveying in Stevens Pass were entertaining. On September 14, 1890, he noted that his survey party was headed for the mountains with good, new tents, a cookstove and plenty of food and would not return until the snows. By December, he reported cheerfully that it was "almost a year since I started out for the wild and woolly west. Have had lots of adventures & have managed to pay expenses at least, and keep a shirt on the baby."

As Haskell had moved through the West (he had formerly worked in Montana), he had speculated a bit in property and had made a modest profit. He wrote his wife that he would like to settle down in the Wenatchee country, and in a letter of January 25, 1891, told her that although the farmers were plowing and the weather was warm and summerlike, something was missing:

> It is lonesome without my pet, and I would like to be home a little while. . . . If you conclude you could endure this kind of a life and it seems best to move here I think it would be best to buy 80 or 160 acres of land build a house & have a place. . . . You would doubtless miss the church work and privileges you have been accustomed to.

By June 1891, the survey party was at Camp Stevens Pass, with most preliminary work completed. They began to lay out the route; by July, they had determined where the necessary tunnel (believed to be the Martin Creek tunnel) should be constructed and were moving to a lower elevation. Haskell had bought five acres at Sultan City for $225, apparently a speculative purchase, and 160 acres on Mission Creek (where Cashmere lies today), about one and a half miles from the Wenatchee River. His later letters were full of his plans for transporting his family to the Wenatchee area.

Once his surveying and locating work for the route through Stevens Pass was completed, Haskell went into business in Wenatchee and later was employed by the U.S. Army Corps of Engineers, working on improvements in navigation for boats traveling the Columbia River between Wenatchee and the Okanogan River. Tragically, he drowned on the Columbia on May 20, 1905.

Meanwhile, James J. Hill moved swiftly to extend the rails to Wenatchee and westbound over Stevens Pass. Feverish land speculation ensued all along the route, especially at Wenatchee, Cashmere, and Leavenworth. Hundreds and then thousands of laborers were organized into orderly crews as work progressed into the Cascades.

5. RAILS WESTWARD

While the surveyors put the final touches on plans for the Cascades, rail crews intensively worked westward from Spokane. Among their early projects was building a bridge across the Columbia below Wenatchee, at Rock Island. Until it was completed, trains had to cross the river by cable ferry.

During the period when vast amounts of lumber were cut for use as trestles, ties, and building materials, loggers harvested Entiat Valley. The logs were placed in the Columbia River, but at Rock Island the problem was how to stop them on the swift-flowing stream. Contractor A. R. Porter summoned from Michigan an experienced crew of river-drivers who soon corralled the logs into booms at the Wenatchee mill.

Two bridges were thrown across the Wenatchee River. In October 1892, near Mission (now Cashmere) the newly completed second bridge collapsed. The locomotive had just cleared the bridge when three cars loaded with rails and workmen plummeted from the overburdened bridge into the river. A fourth car proceeded to hang precariously from the damaged trestle and dump its load on top of the wreck below. Of fourteen workmen who went down with the cars, only six survived.

Crews were deployed along the Wenatchee River, clearing, grading, and finally laying rails. Using horse and mule teams, Fresno scrapers, and hand tools, workmen slogged along. The Fresno scraper was a tricky tool to manage. Usually the team consisted of four mules or horses, urged to do right by the blistering language of the team's driver. The driver held the scraper's lever under his arm until he had a load of dirt or rock; then he moved to the dumping spot and quickly heaved upward on the handle. The cutting edge would stall in the dirt and dump the scraper forward. When it fell back, the driver had to be sure to get his feet out of harm's way.

It was rough and lonely work. An old-timer remembered letting off steam in 1891 at a big dance held at Miller and Freer's store. In *Wenatchee World* reporter Eva Anderson's book *Rails Across the Cascades*, Jack Richardson of Monitor recalled his family's apparent lack of concern that his father's job involved hauling dynamite by horse and wagon from Wenatchee to the construction camps. He remembered the townspeople's excitement when the first trains came through town, and his crushing disappointment at being left behind as "too little" when his brothers got to ride a work train to Wenatchee and back.

Camps mushroomed to house workers: the single in bunkhouses, the married in small homes. There were mess halls, a timekeeper's office, a foreman's office, metal water tanks, and feeding racks for the horses. Many forces drained the workmen: snowslides and rockslides, irate rattlesnakes dislodged by construction in the lower foothills, a searing sun at midsummer and bitter cold in winter, sheer loneliness from the isolation, and the uncertainty of continued employment (if a worker's skills were no longer needed, he would be promptly let go). Yet the work went ahead quite swiftly, considering the difficult terrain.

Mistakes were made, however. As crews started into Tumwater Canyon, natives observed that the river occasionally rose higher than rails were being laid. The crews went ahead with the surveyors' routing, only to have to move the rails to a higher elevation a few years later.

Today, a century later, archaeologists have discovered domelike structures along Tumwater Canyon, similar to those near rail construction sites elsewhere in the West. Often erroneously associated with Chinese workers, the structures were ovens more likely used by the thousands of rail workers of Italian and Greek descent. Indeed, old photos show large, five-by-eight-foot beehive ovens in use. A construction-camp cook built a roaring fire inside the rock enclosure, then removed the coals, inserted bread dough on long paddles, and soon took out dozens of loaves of irresistible crusty bread.

After conquering the gloomy, precipitous ten-mile canyon, which was prone to rockslides and which curved like a snake, the tracklayers had a relatively easy time of it, except for clearing the towering trees obstructing the survey line. From Chiwaukum at the head of Tumwater, the line continued westward along a grade that averaged 1 percent and never exceeded 2.2 percent, through dense forests along Nason Creek—although there were, of course, a few deep canyons to be spanned and ridges to be tunneled.

Horace C. Henry, a subcontractor for the Great Northern Railroad on the western section, energetically turned his talents to the logistics problem of supplying the workers. At that time, supplies were brought from Seattle by steamers that plied the Snohomish River upstream as far as possible, then were transferred to the shallow-draft stern-wheeler *Monte Cristo* as far as Sultan. From there, freight was delivered up-canyon by teams and wagons over horrible roads. Henry attacked the problem with his customary verve and built a shallow-draft stern-wheeler of his own, the *Florence Henry*, that could navigate the river farther up-stream, thus reducing the wagon freight time.

Thousands of horses and mules at construction sites had to be fed, too. According to a biography of Henry by Noble Hoggson, Henry employed a teenager, Josh Green, to haul hay and grain from Skagit Valley farms to be transported upriver. (Green later became president of the Peoples National Bank.)

Henry was a blunt man who brooked no half-baked advice from the GNR's office, halfway across the continent. Hoggson quotes him as curtly informing the office, "If you think you know more about the work out here than I do, you are mistaken." When the St. Paul office asked him to send the company's funds to the home office for safekeeping during the 1893 depression, Henry blithely replied, "You take care of the funds there, I'll take care of them here." He knew the funds would never be seen again in the West but would instead be used to cover the home office's debts. Nevertheless, Henry seemed to be highly regarded for his contracting work.

One of the few personal accounts of workmen on the job was that of W. S. "Will" Dulmage. For a 1970 *Frontier Times* article, Victor H. White interviewed Dulmage, who began working for the GNR on September 25, 1891. Just short of eighteen years of age, Dulmage progressed swiftly from general laborer to fireman within a few days (the regular fireman was drunk and unable to go out on a westbound train loaded with steel rails and supplies). He learned to spread each shovel of coal carefully, instead of dumping it in a heap, as the brand-new "Big Hog," a 404 locomotive, steamed across the eastern Washington scablands. The first stop, where his shoulders must have been aching and where he was covered with coal dust, was Rock Island, just below Wenatchee. There a hot shower and good meal awaited the crew. On past Wenatchee, which at that time consisted of just three dwellings, a railroad station, and a half-finished section house, the train started uphill toward Leavenworth. At Leavenworth the sleek locomotive's load was lightened, and it continued to Cascade Tunnel [Cascade City] station. Dulmage and the engineer (a man named McDougall), buddies by then, wearily climbed the many steps leading to the large section house at Cascade Tunnel, where food awaited. The two crewmen ate and showered there, but slept back in the cab of the locomotive. There they remained on call twenty-four hours a day, manning a second engine to push laden cars uphill, moving cars to different points—gypsies of the railroad for the next six months straight, but making $300 a month, enormous wages for the time (of course, they had nowhere to spend it).

As rails were laid, the locomotive and its crew roamed from Leavenworth to Wellington on the west, hauling, pushing, and pulling. Dulmage told White there were unbelievable amounts of snow from October to May:

> The snow would start coming down in flakes the size of a silver dollar and pile up ten or twelve feet in a night. We would find the track in a twenty-foot deep valley scooped out with snow ploughs or, more often, with 200 men heaving shovels. The temperature would drop. We would keep dry kindling in little makeshift sheds and start fires on the tracks to get the ice thawed enough to throw the switches.

Originally a camp called Stevens City, Wellington was a wide-open town where easy women rode free on the trains to ease the loneliness of construction workers. While the locomotive was parked there awaiting further orders, Dulmage picked up additional money by playing the piano in bars, earning tips from both the house and the women.

The stretch from Wellington toward Scenic, a particularly precipitous area (part of which is now accessible to hikers as the Iron Goat Trail), was west of the summit. Although the towns were only about four air miles apart, the convoluted track between them racked up ten to twelve difficult miles. Dulmage described this area as "saturated with mud, snow and ice all winter and dripping with run-off water and mud most of the summer."

Before the completion of the line and institution of regular service from St. Paul to Seattle, a mixed passenger and freight train ran regularly each way from Spokane to Leavenworth and, as track permitted, on west. The trains carried construction workers, supervisors, and a few of the general public. The GNR's management tacitly permitted train crews to run small ventures on the side. Working as a brakeman in 1892, Dulmage accepted unofficial fares from passengers wanting to avoid the $12 fare from Spokane to Leavenworth—settling them on open flatcars, gondolas, or boxcars.

Construction spawned the growth of several small communities

Artist's drawing of the Great Northern Railroad switchbacks (Photo: North Central Washington Museum, Wenatchee, WA)

besides Leavenworth, the GNR's divisional headquarters until 1922. Along the rail line grew such camps as Merritt, Wellington, Scenic, and Skykomish, then the western terminus of the Cascade Division. (See Chapter 6 for details on these small settlements.)

From Skykomish the GNR continued oceanward along the south fork of the Skykomish River, with bridges across the Skykomish and Miller rivers, to Index and on down to Everett.

Mere words make the feat sound simple; it was not. The terrain on both sides of the summit was too rugged to permit wandering in large loops to create an easy grade. Locomotives of the time were not powerful enough to control trains over the 4 percent grade required to breach the summit. Engineers realized from the beginning that a tunnel would be required but, wanting to plunge into operation as soon as possible, decided to conquer the summit by switchbacks until a tunnel could be built.

Eight switchbacks did the job—five on the west side, three on the east. During construction there was one more at Martin Creek, and a Y track to turn trains around near the summit—both discontinued after the Horseshoe Tunnel was finished. It was a zigzag way to climb a mountain too perpendicular for any other practicable means—like being cradled in a large, ascending rocking chair. The original switchback portion extended 12.15 miles, including the spurs, climbing 6.4 miles from Tunnel City (later Cascade Tunnel station) on the east side to go through Stevens Pass at a 4,055-foot altitude. It descended 5.75 miles to Wellington. On the east side sufficient workable terrain permitted curvature of the track with no more than a 3.5 percent grade using three spurs. The west side was steeper and required five spurs of as much as 4 percent grade to rock the trains down. Part of today's Pacific Crest Trail follows the old switchback roadbed, north of Stevens Pass.

The curves themselves were exciting. Some were twelve to thirteen degrees. There was a constant ten-degree curve to complete the 180-degree reversal along Martin Creek (Horseshoe Tunnel); in order to make the steep descent westward, the train had to enter and exit a mountainside.

Two locomotives puffed ahead of a typical seven-car passenger train, with one attached backward to the last car to pull the train along the switchback spur. Freights up to eighteen cars had to split up and go over the top in two segments. The train went forward on 1,000-foot spurs. When the locomotive reached the end of the spur, the train reversed direction up another spur, and so on over the pass. Some trains made the trip backwards.

Just the matter of supplying the several hundred men working in both directions, living in crude bunkhouses or rough-cut homes with their families, required immense logistical planning. Everything from groceries to children's toys was carried and catalogued for delivery to the right camps. No surprise, then, that when two trains collided near Monitor one year, a bonanza of items was scattered along the tracks and gleefully carted off by local children and adults. Another wreck in the same area left bundles of shingles floating down the Wenatchee River.

Despite the obstacles, the work got done. After two years, in the early morning of January 6, 1893, workmen still had 9,000 feet of rail to lay near Scenic. Incredibly, they completed the job by 8:00 P.M. that day. Bundled up and standing in deep snow, Superintendent Cornelius Shields and District Superintendent J. D. Farrell pounded in the last spike by lantern light. A GNR press release, issued in 1968 to commemorate the seventy-fifth anniversary of the crossing completion, described the event this way:

> Snow was piled high at trackside in the Cascade Mountains 75 years ago on January 6, 1893, when two Great Northern Railway officials drove the final spike into a roughly-hewn crosstie. . . . Pomp and ceremony was

ignored as workmen on the track-laying rig lowered the last rail onto the ties. . . . As the heavy maul pounded the last spike, cheers rose from the workmen. They were drowned out by sharp cracks from a six-shooter and the shrill whistles of work train locomotives.

The first through train rolled into Seattle on January 8, 1893, but scheduled service began with a train that left Minneapolis for Tacoma on June 15.

The stations on the Stevens Pass portion at this time included, east to west: Mission (now Cashmere), Peshastin, Leavenworth, Chiwaukum, Nason Creek (today the ghost town of Winton), Merritt, Berne, Cascade Tunnel, and Cascade Summit; then Wellington, Scenic (still called Madison?), Skykomish, and Index. After the Cascade Tunnel opened in 1900, the stations were Leavenworth, Tumwater, Drury, Chiwaukum, Nason Creek, Merritt, Gaynor, Berne, Cascade Tunnel; then Wellington, Scenic, Skykomish, and Index. There were several other flag stops, too.

Passengers considered the Cascades crossing a true adventure. Every effort was made to minimize danger. All parts of the train were examined before the passage. To clear the heavy winter snows from tracks, two powerful locomotives were hooked up back to back with rotary snowplows at each end. The contraption worked back and forth across the mountain, returning to the starting point. With slides and avalanches always possible, snow crews drew double pay, and many were stationed at Cascade City and Wellington.

Significant accidents were rare, but in her book *Trails Across the Cascades* Eva Anderson quoted an early engineer, Ernest Spencer, who said the trip was always memorable and seemed endless. Spencer marveled at the Horseshoe Tunnel. The GNR track went over a bridge trestle across the river; the rails then intruded into the mountainside at a ten-degree constant curve and then came back out, parallel to where they had started. Spencer verified that, as he emerged from the tunnel, he could look out the locomotive window and see the end of his train going in.

There were times when the snowplow crew was unable to keep ahead of the snowfall, which on occasion was as much as twelve inches per hour. Anderson quoted a man named Herbert Ogden who, with his mother and three siblings, was aboard a train in January 1897 that became stalled on the switchbacks for fifty-six hours. Extra help was rushed from the west to shovel and scrape but, as soon as the train could move forward to another segment, it hit more snow and literally froze to the tracks. Ogden said a traveling salesman aboard entertained the passengers with his guitar and got them all singing to pass the scary time.

While the switchbacks enabled trains to run through to Puget Sound

Despite the Great Northern Railroad's best efforts, wrecks occurred along the line. (Photo: North Central Washington Museum, Wenatchee, WA)

and tap the burgeoning Orient trade, the costs of crossing were high compared to the rail traffic of the time. In 1896, the GNR moguls gave approval to start a tunnel through the Cascades—while continuing to use the switchbacks for uninterrupted operations.

Actually, the GNR's John F. Stevens had partially surveyed the line for such a tunnel himself during an earlier exploration trip. After both Cascade Tunnel portals were established, surveyors built roofed towers over transits, high above the terrain at each end of the projected tunnel. In line above the projected tunnel route were two mountain peaks, one of 1,750 feet and the other of 2,150 feet. Extending higher than snow, two-inch gas pipes (protected from the elements by timber encasements or towers) formed transit targets. Instead of using any triangulation, surveyors could simply keep the tunnel in line with the four targets thus established. Inside the tunnel, workmen built a double-floored platform near the ceiling to support transits and transitmen, thus maintaining an accurate centerline as the excavation progressed.

Work began on August 10, 1897. A crew of 400 to 600 men working at each portal removed rock and debris, the new advance was buttressed, and a new dig was begun. Sometimes the hole moved forward only one foot per day, yet it averaged 350 feet per month. Sweaty, muscled men removed debris—dirt, boulders, and rock that had been drilled and blasted loose—from the excavation, hauling it by wheelbarrow onto a massive traveling platform dubbed "Jumbo." The device incorporated chutes that were opened to dump the muck into railcars. Entire boulders went onto flatcars. Special heavy-duty electric motors pulled up to twenty cars of one-cubic-yard capacity outside for disposal. There men separated rock suitable for use (after reduction) in concrete from general scrap, installing the mixing equipment on a hillside above each portal, so that wet concrete could be sent to railcars by gravity. The tunnel was reinforced with concrete two to three and a half feet thick. While finishers lined and smoothed a 500-foot segment, others prepared a second segment to receive the concrete, streamlining and speeding the operation. The portal archways extended about 200 feet from each portal to minimize snow problems at those points.

The eastern and western excavation crews finally met inside the Cascades on September 23, 1900. Despite the project's having used surveying methods that modern-day contractors would consider primitive, alignment of the two sections of tunnel, both horizontally and vertically, was less than an inch off in a tunnel of 13,813 feet, or approximately two and a half miles.

According to calculations by W. C. Hartranft of the Great Northern Railway Historical Society, the Cascade Tunnel saved 8.54 miles and eliminated 2,332 degrees of curvature. There was some new track required to reroute traffic through the tunnel, but it was not extensive. The new tunnel route opened on December 10, 1900. It ran from Cascade Tunnel, a construction-camp settlement on the east (now the site of the Yodelin ski area), to Wellington, today a ghost-town site in the canyon below Stevens Pass Highway as it descends westbound. The maintenance crews rejoiced in the realization that no longer would accumulations of 140 feet of snow (as in the winter of 1897–98) have to be removed at the switchbacks' summit.

6. CONSTRUCTION CAMP SETTLEMENTS

The Great Northern Railroad established camps at convenient points along the projected rail line in order to house and feed the workers laboring on its projects: first the rights-of-way and tracks toward Stevens Pass, then the Cascade switchbacks, the Cascade Tunnel, and later, from 1925 to 1928, the Eight-Mile Tunnel. After the railroad work was completed, the camps became scheduled stops for the local trains, inhabited by those who still worked on the railroad or in local mills. Each settlement averaged one or two hundred residents in the early century. From east to west, they were:

Chiwaukum was near the point where the Wenatchee River entered Tumwater Canyon. Thomas J. Dillon homesteaded near Chiwaukum in 1892 and was married the year after. Despite the scarcity of pasture there, he managed to assemble a profitable stock ranch. In 1893, Frank and Henry Middleton installed a mill on a GNR sidetrack. Frank was killed in a mill accident, but Henry continued to operate the mill until 1902, when he sold it to Frank Dorn and Norman Titchenal. The town also had a store and hotel. A fish hatchery thrived for a time.

Winton was first called Woodspur, then Nason, by the railroad crews. Possibly the first settlers of Winton were the T. J. Dillon, Jr., and Richard F. Dillon families, soon joined by Richard Giblin, a relative. As a railroad camp, it was as tough as any other. An old newspaper account tells of a con man working the Nason Creek camp: "Black Jack," who played the old "nut shell game," was shot by a disgruntled patron or competitor and buried somewhere along Stevens Pass under a weeping fir tree that some called the "umbrella tree." The camp had more unrest when, in 1905 at Bartlett & Hogan's log camp, one intoxicated man stabbed another in the stomach.

C. A. Harris and his son Arden operated a mill from 1914 to 1916, making ties for the Great Northern Lumber Company. Harris apparently moved his equipment around to take advantage of lumber needs, for in 1883 he had a sawmill on Badger Mountain east of the Columbia, in 1892 he was in Entiat, and after leaving Winton in 1917, he built a sawmill in the Entiat Valley again, naming the settlement growing up around the mill Ardenvoir.

There was also a Sampson's Grocery Company in Winton, but after being sold to A. D. Allen and then to a man named Nichols, it burned down. Today there is a Longview Fibre Company mill at Winton.

Merritt was a post office and flag station. Widow Inez Forsyth and her seven children filed on 160 acres of heavily timbered land at Merritt in 1892. The plucky woman built a wooden cabin chinked with moss and mud for her brood's first winter. How she made a living is unknown, but perhaps she sold her timber. Her children rode horseback to a one-room school that was later demolished in a snowslide. Education was important to Forsyth, who sent her children to Leavenworth for high school, where they worked for room and board at residents' homes. Two of her daughters went on to college, particularly unusual for young women of the time.

After her children were adults, Forsyth operated a boardinghouse in Leavenworth, where she met and married barber Thomas William Greave. The couple moved back to Merritt to open the Merritt Inn on Forsyth's land. It was a family affair, with Greave barbering the customers and Inez's daughter Millie cooking and operating the post office that existed there until 1943. When a drifter offered to work for his keep, Forsyth supervised his building of several cabins to augment the lodgings, and added another log building as a restaurant and grocery. Some U.S. Forest Service personnel believe that the bark exteriors of the cabins came from Stevens Pass, because old trees peeled of bark have been found there. The Merritt Inn stayed in business to an extent until the 1950s. Millie later married a man named Otis Marsh; she died in 1959. The inn burned down around 1980, leaving only two large brick fireplace remnants visible from the highway.

Ellen and Alexander Porter came to Merritt in 1892. Alexander Porter, a camp cook, was killed by a train shortly thereafter while crossing the river on a railroad bridge. Meanwhile, H. B. Smith had come to work for the GNR in 1896, living at a camp near Merritt next to Porter's 160-acre claim. Smith married Porter in 1899, and filed on an eighty-acre claim next to hers. When Smith's work on the Cascade Tunnel was completed, the couple stayed on in the wilderness, trading and trapping furs for a living.

In 1904, H. B. Smith built the eight-bedroom Merritt Hotel, and later a small grocery, catering to railroad men and transient sheepherders. When hikers and fishermen began coming to the area, they too stayed at the hotel. During the winter of 1906, a train was stalled from slides for several days; the Smiths housed and fed the passengers and crew when the train's supplies gave out, receiving the personal thanks and generous repayment of James J. Hill himself.

Often residents of the area walked the railroad track as the easiest path through the dense woods. When rotary plows threw up huge drifts of snow on either side during winter, however, walking the track was dangerous. It took the life of Samuel Hawkins, a prospector headed to the mountains from Merritt, when he was trapped in such a deep cut and fell backwards trying to climb away from the oncoming train.

Berne was a listed station on the GNR, but before construction began on the Eight-Mile Tunnel, the only person living there was a track walker, bachelor David Brown. There was a depot located on the main line, and later a second one about 100 yards east of the west switch. Located at the east portal of the new tunnel, Berne was an important camp after the mid-1920s, but it was burned after the tunnel construction was completed. As late as the 1950s, though, a "watchman," Thelma Kasophous, was stationed alone at Berne (her husband was gone all day on a section crew). Her job was to staff a work station consisting of a phone line and two handles, one red and one green. Upon receiving instructions from GNR Skykomish, she pulled the proper handle to activate or deactivate the power to the tunnel's catenary system.

Cascade Tunnel was also known as Tunnel City and Cascade City, the latter during the laying of the original switchback rails in the 1890s. It was a way station then, and later was home to workmen starting on the Cascade Tunnel. Several hundred men, mostly single, lived in bunkhouses and homes there, prompting some Leavenworth merchants to open branch stores. Businesses included Charles Scherinewski's restaurant, Robert Dye's barbershop, and Frank Dorn's merchandise store. Saloons were heavily patronized. A sensational *New York World* article dubbing Cascade Tunnel the wickedest place in the world was picked up by newspapers as far away as London. In June 1900, local resident Frank Reeves defended his town as being wicked, yes, but hardly the wickedest in the world, since one deputy sheriff was able to monitor the 500 people, mostly male laborers, living there.

The town's morals became academic later that month, when a fire burned every business building, all of them frame structures. Since the need for a town at Cascade Tunnel had largely disappeared with the completion of the tunnel that year, the settlement soon fell into near-oblivion. By 1910, it consisted only of a small depot, a few railroad spurs, a turntable, a water tank, an electric substation, a shelter for the electric engines, and a few workers' cabins. The cookhouse, which served residents and passing crewmen, was just a kitchen and crude dining room with a dozen or so tables and benches.

Mill Creek camp was a settlement that existed during the Eight-Mile Tunnel construction.

Wellington was perched on the hill and straggled along a small valley just outside the western end of the Cascade Tunnel. It was named for a GNR investor. First construction workers and then railroad crews and maintenance people populated the small town, originally named Stevens City. Because of its strategic location, it was the headquarters for electric-motor work on the small engines towing trains through the Cascade Tunnel, as well as for tunnel maintenance. There were three spurs near the tunnel and, a few hundred feet west, two sidetracks and passing tracks, a coal shed, and a water tank. A small depot, roadmaster's office, section house, and crew bunkhouse and cookhouse completed the railroad facilities. In winter several dozen shovelers, those who manually cleared the tracks of rocks and snow, called Wellington home.

Wellington was renamed Tye after the disastrous avalanche of 1910, the GNR not wanting to remind its passengers of such dire potential consequences of riding its trains. (See Chapter 7 for the saga.)

During the construction and operation of Cascade Tunnel, as many as 600 people, mostly men, lived in Wellington/Tye. Among them were Ben Nowak, who came in 1913 to work as a GNR brakeman, and his brother Ed, who came in 1921 and who was also a brakeman for the GNR. Wellington/Tye was where crews changed locomotives, or hooked up electric helper engines for the tunnel trip, and it had a fairly spacious rail yard. Life as a brakeman was hazardous: the job involved running along the top of a boxcar, jumping across to the next car, and using an axe handle to turn the brakes. Once John Finn, a Nowak family relative, left to go to a family funeral on a train that wound up plunging into the Skykomish River, killing the brakeman and injuring the engineer but no one else.

With lonely, often transient workmen the chief settlers in the mountain camps, one could expect trouble. Perhaps, like Cascade Tunnel, Tye was not any more wicked than any other camp, but isolation certainly made men short-tempered. In November 1913, William Hurst and Thomas Brannon, roommates in a crude shack, got into a fight that ranged through the town. Hurst told authorities that Brannon and he quarreled and he stamped out to walk away, whereupon Brannon and a friend followed him, taunting him until Hurst turned to give Brannon a thrashing. The friend pitched in, too, and Hurst eventually pulled a knife and sliced through his roommate's jugular vein. A train passing through just happened to have a detective on board, who arrested Hurst and took him to Leavenworth, charging him with murder.

But families survived in this wilderness; both Nowak brothers raised their families in Tye. Some present-day residents of the Northwest, all related, who remember living there as children are Mary Ren, Marilyn Carter, Delwyn Nowak (Ed Nowak's son), and Kathleen Mankin (John Finn's daughter). One of their relatives, Ira E. Clary, lived through the Wellington avalanche of 1910 and later served as superintendent of the Western District for the GNR at Everett.

Children's lives in Tye were a bit like that of Huck Finn. They wore overalls and, in summer, went barefoot. They could fish for steelhead in the Skykomish River and, when fishing waned, swim in the Beckler River nearby. They knew every train and its crew the way today's children know baseball and football team members. With little exposure to the outside world, most families were quite healthy. For childbirth, though, women took the train to Everett about three weeks before an expected birth. Marilyn Carter's mother helped to deliver a baby who was too eager to enter the world; born to the Colgren family in 1925, it was the only baby known to have been born at Tye.

When Carter was growing up, Tye consisted of only twenty-five or thirty houses and Vincent Boozer's general store, with a building attached housing Bailet's Hotel upstairs and a restaurant downstairs. Mrs. Bailet ran the restaurant, cured her own meats, baked pies and bread, cooked, and waited on tables. She managed to make Bailet's a cheerful place, with curtains at the windows and blue- and red-checkered tablecloths. From the porch, patrons could easily watch train traffic emerge from the west portal of the tunnel. Next door was a pool hall owned by Joe Boozer.

Living in Tye in winter was unique. All the buildings were connected by covered snowsheds, for winter snows often came to the eaves of homes. The back doors opened into the snowsheds, which were roofed over and had boarded sides and floors spaced apart a little. "You went out there to go to the store, to go to school, and even to visit the outhouses," Carter recalls. "As a small child, I could not go into the snowsheds alone at night because wolves occasionally wandered into them." Wolves and bears were common then in the mountains, the eerie pack howlings a part of daily life. Coyotes and deer often became trapped in the deep snow ruts made by the snowplows, and would frantically try to escape.

There were about ten Japanese men living in Tye in the 1920s and 1930s, working as section hands. Every Christmas they delivered a box of tangerines to each home. Carter recalls:

> We were all one family in Tye. The Japanese were kind to us. They fed me raw fish with chopsticks, and on the Fourth of July, the Japanese were the only ones that seemed to have any fireworks. Tye had a good baseball team, including the Japanese, and competed against other camps.

Carter says sheepherders and flocks came through Tye bound for the high country. Her mother often sent a coconut cake to the herders; sure enough, the following day they would send down a lamb from the mountains.

The big social event of the day was the arrival of the one o'clock train, bringing groceries and mail and special items from the Sears Roebuck catalog. Delwyn Nowak recalls that the men drank and gambled, mostly at poker, when off duty. When life got too boring, the residents pooled their money and hired a band to come to Tye on the train. Everyone attended, dancing all night in the school gym, while the children slept on benches. Camp families could ride the local train to Skykomish any time at no charge. Adults called it the Dinky, but Kathleen Mankin recalls that the children called it the Dingbat.

When fire started in the company housing at Tye in July 1926, it spread like wildfire through the tunnels of the snowsheds, covered with tar paper, that connected homes, burning the homes or goods of fourteen families. Most families could not save anything except what furniture they could lug outside away from the sheds. Mankin's family "got everything out of the house, but it burned where it sat. Everything went up in flames except the piano." Ben Nowak dynamited the main snowshed, stopping the spread of the fire and saving some of the homes. For a time the bereft moved in with their neighbors.

When the Eight-Mile Tunnel was opened in 1928, most of the families moved to Berne, at the eastern end of the new tunnel. Others, like Mankin's parents, the John Finns, moved to Skykomish. The remains of Tye sank into the underbrush; the tunnels gradually filled with earth from slides, and the snowsheds collapsed.

Martin City was near the junction of Deception Creek and the Tye River. It existed for only about two years around 1892–93, during the construction of the GNR, but it was a very lively place for railroad crews to let off steam. An old photo shows a movie house, a restaurant, taverns, and what probably were bawdy houses.

Scenic, first called Madison, was at first little more than a water tower and depot managed by a telegraph operator and his wife. It was located at the top of a considerable downgrade to Skykomish. It was not unusual for an eastbound train to be held up at little Scenic while some trouble ahead was cleared. Furnishing relaxation for transient rail workers were five brothels between Scenic and Skykomish, among them the Onion Patch, the Red Wagon, and the Mouse's Ear.

The introduction to life was rough in the wintry Cascades. In December 1909, an astonished track walker found a newborn baby, perfectly nude, lying near the tracks by Scenic. He hustled it into town, where local women clothed it and awaited developments. Before long, word came from Leavenworth that Dr. Hoxsey had received a young woman off the train for postdelivery care, and that the distraught woman had said that her baby had been delivered in the "closet," or bathroom, of the train and had fallen clear through to the tracks. The baby had lain there about twenty to thirty minutes, but it was no worse for its chilly entrance into the world.

A highly respectable resort accommodating up to 100 guests, the green and white Scenic Hot Springs Hotel, was built in 1904 by Joseph V.

A dance at Scenic Hot Springs Hotel drew throngs of railroad workers and their girlfriends or wives. (Photo: Special Collections Division, University of Washington Libraries, neg. Pickett 3264)

Prosser, reportedly at a cost of $30,000. It was widely touted by magazines and newspapers for its splendid location and facilities. *The Seattle Mail and Herald* of August 4, 1906, reported that the hotel was furnished in oak and had electric lights, steam heat, call bells, and the best of dining-room service. Guests could play billiards, lawn tennis, handball, croquet, and basketball. They could hike and fish as well as enjoy the hot baths on the lower floor of the hotel. There were separate quarters for men and women. The newspaper described Prosser as a man who might have said, "I will carve here in the wilderness a spot where the weary may find rest, where the sick may get well, where the nerve-strained denizens of the outer world may find . . . quietness and healing." Other reports pointed to the delights of Deception Falls and Surprise Falls. A mile above the latter falls, a foaming hot sulfur spring issued from beneath a giant rock (the water was then piped down to the hotel).

Unfortunately, the hotel burned during the Christmas holidays of 1908. The guests all got out safely, but they lost everything. Proprietor J. V. Prosser was severely burned trying unsuccessfully to save his personal papers. The new hotel reopened on June 5, 1909, with a Swiss chalet mode of architecture. There were sixty rooms, including six suites with private baths, furnished comfortably. The hot baths were still located on the lower floor. The train stopped only 300 feet away. Passengers alighting from the train were awed by the hotel's setting in a deep valley, almost encircled by snow-covered peaks. Since the area received three to five feet of snow and was just a four-hour train ride from the city, it was a popular winter-sports destination for Seattleites of the time. During construction of the Eight-Mile Tunnel, Scenic's population swelled dramatically with workers, since the town was very near the western portal. On October 27, 1927, residents and hotel guests enjoyed a major prizefight held at Scenic between Jack Humphrey and Kid Kelly.

Unfortunately, the popular old resort was in line with the relocation of the GNR through the Eight-Mile Tunnel, and the site was literally covered up with earth. Today some of the old construction houses are still being used, and a small new housing development has brought in a few new residents.

Nippon was probably a camp for Japanese workers building the GNR in the 1890s, but in 1903 its name was changed to Alpine. Yet on June 16, 1907, the Nippon Lumber Company at Alpine was organized by George W. Fairchild, W. O. Clemans, and C. L. Clemans, the latter having been captain of Stanford University's first football team. The new firm intended to build a sawmill with a daily capacity of 10,000 board feet. Two years later, the Clemans brothers acquired full interest in the

Alpine (earlier known as Nippon) was the site of the Alpine Lumber Company and its company town. (Photo: Special Collections Division, University of Washington Libraries, neg. Pickett 3040 B)

firm and built a mill by April 1910. The plant made an average daily cut of about 30,000 board feet. The firm's chief business at the time was producing 12x12s for snowsheds. The company town boasted a population of 200. In 1913, the mill burned but was promptly rebuilt in record time. Fire threatened again from burning slash nearby the following year, and the company's logging railroad trestles were destroyed, a considerable and inconvenient loss. On July 18, 1917, the plant did burn down but was rebuilt by September, equipped this time with an automatic sprinkler system. Between 1910 and 1914, the mill's annual output of lumber and shingles went from 150 cars to 508 cars; after that time, the shipments stabilized at about 600 cars annually.

Management seems to have been benevolent, sponsoring company picnics and annual banquets. Workers' rent, heat, and water were free, and the company store had liberal credit terms. Despite the isolation (there was no road at all), snows reaching to fifteen feet deep, and interrupted communications during bad weather, the residents seemed happy. Everything and everybody came and went by the GNR, the tracks bisecting the town. Houses were heated by wood stoves, and driving winter snows sometimes left a mist of snow on bedclothes of a morning. Running water came from a trough on the back porch. Yet workers considered the mill a fine place to work, and they would assault representatives of the IWW (the Wobblies) who came to organize them.

Many children in town enjoyed skiing across the railroad trestles or swinging on knotted ropes over the canyons (against their parents' wishes). The town had a school of its own, too. One of the teachers there from 1919 to the early 1930s was Jane Farnham, who honeymooned with her new husband at Martin Creek—"hooking" a freight train for the short ride. In a 1978 talk covered by the Wenatchee World, Farnham, who came from Iowa to teach in Alpine, shared her initial impressions of the town with the Chelan County Heritage Committee:

> You can't imagine what it was like to step off the train at Alpine—a lumber camp on a steep hill. Ferns stood as high as I did. Chimneys stuck out of the undergrowth. I wondered what I was doing there, but life with a capital "L" began at Alpine. Carl "Papa" Clemans had a monopoly on the town, owning everything but the depot and dance hall. He was a kindly man who once bought the wedding dress and flowers for a bride, gave free Thanksgiving dinners for all the residents, and fed any traveler. Clemans' grocery was a true general store, selling everything from logging shoes to silk stockings, eggs and butter.

Farnham taught Alpine's high school students in a two-room school, and had to obtain a working knowledge of business subjects and foreign languages. She found Alpine to be a close-knit community where even a respectable woman could go into the pool hall to buy ice cream or candy without censure. The town was not free of accidents, though. Farnham told of a railcar, carrying a load of steel and an undetermined amount of dynamite, which had gotten loose from the train and had plummeted westward. Had it not jumped a trestle, it would have collided with an eastbound freight out of Skykomish. A freight train got stuck one day in Horseshoe Tunnel, almost suffocating crew members and free-riders before it was cleared. During one winter, the roadbed collapsed and rolled a train into the middle of town, scattering debris and burying a cabin.

Although much of the timber around Alpine was logged off by 1928, Security Timber Company bought the Nippon Lumber Company that year and expanded. Security established a camp at the big Tonga bridge, where there was a log cabin possibly dating to the Dutch Miller Mining Company days. Soon Security quit too, however, and Alpine's citizens moved away. The U.S. Forest Service later burned the buildings to avoid the hazard of fires being set by squatters or transients taking over the town.

Berlin, about two miles west of Skykomish, was a flag stop. Around 1900, a small sawmill and shingle mill operated, and the Great Republic Gold Mine had its headquarters there. Several other small mining companies kept offices in Berlin, convenient to the myriad claims that spilled over the ridge into the Snoqualmie drainage.

The most promising mine was the Apex, toward Red Mountain and southeast of Lake Elizabeth. Credit for its discovery in 1892 has been afforded in local Skykomish accounts to John Maloney. Mining engineer L. K. Hodges wrote in his book *Mining in the Pacific Northwest*, however, that Alexander McCartney located the mine in 1889; perhaps Maloney bought it from McCartney. In any case, after the GNR was completed in 1893, Maloney brought ore down from the mine by pack train for shipment. A subsequent owner, Abner Griffin, spent $100,000 on development and transportation. The company built a six-mile access railroad to connect with a 3,200-foot tram from the mine, but by the time the locomotive arrived, the rails had become so rusty that on its first run up the steep grade, the locomotive started to slip and slide backward. At a curve it jumped the tracks and overturned. There it sat for years until it was removed for scrap. Following this debacle, Apex used horse teams to pull cars uphill to the mine; when they were filled, they coasted down to the concentrator. Reported return at the smelter was $41.07 per 237-ton shipment.

Berlin's population may have been as large as 500 in 1900, but the site burned down in a 1906 forest fire caused by a spark from a locomotive near town. At first the fire was not taken too seriously, but soon residents began to load possessions onto boxcars and got a locomotive from Skykomish to come and take the cars to Index. Burned were a mine concentrator, a sawmill, a shingle mill, a lath mill, two grocery stores, two hotels, an assay office, a confectionery, five saloons, and thirty houses. Some placed their possessions in the streams, but so fierce was the fire that it burned everything not totally immersed. The only building spared was the Apex barn, which housed most of the townspeople temporarily after the fire. The GNR reimbursed residents for their losses, but most did not rebuild.

A school, a highway department building, and the Miller River Inn and Store, operated by Millard Fillmore Smith and his wife, Esther, constituted Berlin thereafter. Because the name Berlin was embarrassing during World War I, the town changed its name to Miller River. One enduring Berlin landmark is the one-room Miller River School, which served about sixteen pupils in eight grades until 1933. The heyday of mining activity in the area was from 1900 to 1905, although Apex was still operating in a more limited capacity as late as 1920. In 1921–22 the Weyerhaeuser Company donated eighteen acres of land adjacent to Miller River for the lovely Money Creek State Park.

Grotto was the site of a Portland Cement plant that operated for several years after the Depression, helping Skykomish Valley residents to stay in their homes. It also was the site of the Grotto Lumber Company mill.

Baring was barely on the map. (Photo: Special Collections Division, University of Washington Libraries, neg. Pickett 1871)

Baring was called Salmon and then Cosco before it was named Baring, after one of the GNR's financiers. It was little more than a flag stop, consisting originally of a grocery store (in 1926 owned by C. C. Parker), Maloney's Quarry, and Maloney's three-story Grandview Hotel (the word "hotel," early in the century, could also mean a boardinghouse for workers). Soon there was the small Wilder mill and Scripture's Shingle Mill, as well as a couple of saloons and a barbershop. Joyce Timpe, mayor of Skykomish in 1994, recalls her childhood in Baring: "My friend and I used to push a handcart up on Wilder's old logging railroad and ride down the rails." She recalls that the loggers and mill workers of the area took up a collection to bring the Luis Firpo–[Jack] Dempsey fight to Baring, prior to the boxers' world championship contest. Cockfighting and dogfights were popular, too, though illegal—but then, stills in the area turned out potent moonshine as well.

Halford was a regular stop where GNR trains took on water. The GNR also maintained a quarry there for materials used on the roadbed. During the Eight-Mile Tunnel construction period, John Simpson operated an open-air dance hall, restaurant, and tavern at Halford. There was also an Eagle Falls Tavern in the town.

Heybrook had the John Beck Sawmill and a handful of homes.

In addition to the above camps, there were a few small flag stops or depots such as Alvin and Gaynor.

7. ELECTRIFICATION AND THE CASCADE TUNNEL

Whether because of human error or the failure of equipment, signals, or the rails themselves, wrecks were all too common in the early days of the railroad. Contractors provided runaway lanes for the trains—first uphill tracks and then dirt, like those for today's runaway trucks. In fact, for a time, switches were set routinely to the runaway tracks; an engineer had to signal that his train *was* under control before the through switch would be thrown.

At the east end of the Chumstick bridge in April 1904, 250 feet of roadbed collapsed, sending the locomotive and tender of an eastbound train tumbling into the Wenatchee River. The engineer was thrown out but was fatally injured; the fireman was under the wreckage and was scalded besides. Three tramps riding on the tender were crushed beyond recognition. The mail and baggage cars remained upright, and the train engineer Jack Croak's eight-year-old son, riding in the mail car, was uninjured. The other passengers also survived.

An accident five months later left no one injured and everyone laughing. Two men in a locomotive bound for repairs at Leavenworth had just passed Merritt when the air brakes refused to work on the Tumwater downgrade. As the locomotive accelerated, the two crewmen jumped off. After walking about six miles toward Leavenworth, they found the locomotive peacefully puffing away before a short upgrade.

Given the number of Great Northern Railroad trains passing through the Cascades—as many as 300 per month—it's not surprising that accidents and other problems occurred. Despite consistent monitoring of track and slide conditions, trains and lives were lost. In late October 1906, a head-on collision between a freight train and a passenger train between Monroe and Sultan took several crewmen's lives. A newspaper account said that the freight's engineer was literally catapulted through the air from his cab. Faulty communications were to blame.

Snow fell continuously for forty-eight hours in early February 1907, piling up five feet on the level. Trains were stalled for a full week. One eastbound train at Gaynor (on the east side of Stevens Pass) was partially covered by a slide, but rescuers dug out the passengers, who were unhurt. From that point to Cascade Tunnel, observers said there were ten to twenty-five snowslides to the mile. On the west, a track walker reported thirty-nine slides between Skykomish and the tunnel. Rotary snowplows were helpless in many slide conditions, and the GNR employed crews of men, often as many as a hundred per blockage, to shovel out the tracks manually.

Cascade Tunnel also had a knotty ventilation problem, which was evident as soon as it was opened in 1900. Prevailing winds were from the west or southwest, and locomotives struggling uphill from Skykomish, usually one at each end of a train, entered the tunnel belching smoke and gases—which did not escape. Winds changing direction sometimes created a pocket of fumes in a section of the long tunnel.

Even as plans for a solution were being discussed, in 1903 a passenger train became disconnected from its engine accidentally, and the train stopped. Engine crews soon were overcome by smoke, and only the quick action by a fireman riding the train as a passenger prevented the 103 passengers on board from being asphyxiated. He released the locomotive's brakes, and the train, with passenger cars dutifully bumping along behind, rolled to safety outside the tunnel. On November 2, 1906, four section crewmen working in the tunnel were overcome by suffocation. Three were hit by a westbound train before they could be rescued or dragged to safety, while a fourth escaped. These incidents and other narrow escapes accelerated the GNR's plans for using electric engines through the tunnel.

First the company had to obtain a source of power and build the catenary system required. In March 1907, the GNR applied to the U.S. government for the right to construct a dam or dams on the Wenatchee River and to use a 100-foot right-of-way from the power plant to the

Cascade Tunnel for its high-voltage line. Leavenworth was designated as divisional headquarters for the GNR in May 1907. An article in the May 3, 1907, *Leavenworth Echo* indicated just how busy the GNR line through the Cascades was: in April alone, 270 freight trains stopped at the railroad station, each averaging thirty cars. Locally, the Lamb-Davis Lumber Company alone sent out fifteen cars of lumber weekly.

The dam project was placed under the supervision of Robert Herzog, a GNR engineer, and was pushed forward with all haste, due to the acknowledged hazards of the Cascade Tunnel. Within a few months, at least two hundred workmen were distributed from Leavenworth to the dam site in Tumwater Canyon, of which some remains are still visible today near the Alps store. The dam was at the foot of a wide place in the river called Big Lake. Footings thirty-eight feet below the riverbed were excavated to ensure its ability to hold the water trapped as needed behind the 600-foot-long dam. The firm of Caughren & Woldsen began the grading and excavating for an eight-foot, six-inch pipeline to convey water two and a half miles downstream to the powerhouse. The brick powerhouse, 76 by 117 feet, was three stories high and of plain, sturdy design. A twelve-foot excavation was required to bring the feeder pipes into the structure, and large pumps kept the roaring river, a rapids at this point, from inundating workmen. A 210-foot steel tower held the equalization tank in place; this structure, which equalized water pressure so that water pipes would not self-destruct with sudden variations in water flow, held a million gallons of water.

The electrical equipment was installed under the supervision of a Niagara Falls engineer, W. S. Skinner. Equipment was installed to drive a 4,000-horsepower dynamo, providing the three-phase electrical power system needed to drive the trains' engines. This system was considered a bit unusual; it had two wires for the power, with the rails acting as the third "wire," or ground. It was a system used quite widely in Europe but not heretofore in the United States. The *Echo* reported on October 16, 1908:

> There are wires by the hundred, brass and copper and porcelain fixtures by the thousand, to say nothing of iron pipes and castings, and innumerable things large and small that are necessary to the complete working of the plant.

During the winter of 1908, when water was first turned into the powerhouse system, the huge equalization tower collapsed, entailing a loss of $30,000. Its collapse was said to result from a manufacturer's defect.

At the east end of the tunnel, GNR workers built a substation where

Prior to the diesel locomotives used today, big electric locomotives pulled trains over Stevens Pass. (Photo: North Central Washington Museum, Wenatchee, WA)

transformers stepped down the voltage from 6,600 to 2,200 volts. They strung lines to carry the power from substations through the tunnel, from the town of Cascade Tunnel to Wellington, one set on either side of the track so that, if one should fail, the other would suffice. Operations were essentially similar to that of a city streetcar or trolley bus, except that while streetcar systems might tap into about 500 volts, four times that power was available to the 900-ton, General Electric–made electric engines pulling the trains. Each such locomotive was equipped with four motors rated at 375 horsepower. The driving wheels were sixty inches in diameter. Each locomotive was capable of hauling a 1,000-ton train at a speed of fifteen miles per hour on a 2 percent grade. The unique feature was that the motors themselves provided assistance to the air brakes by regeneration of power.

The boxy little electric engines (GE 5000 to 5003), which could handle only about 1,600 tons, had to pull through the tunnel both the steam locomotives, puffing only enough to avoid being a drag, and the cars. At Wellington, the electrics were uncoupled and the steam locomotives took over for the trip west. The electrification would expand later. As freight trains became longer in the mid-1920s, two electric engines no longer supplied sufficient power to move the trains over the grade and through the tunnel. Furthermore, the Tumwater power plant's output could not cope with the power requirements of three or four pushers/pullers at once. Therefore, for some years the freights had to be broken in two and hauled over the grades in "installments," a costly process. Engineers designed a special traction connector that enabled the engines to operate at seven and a half instead of fifteen miles per hour, drawing less current and making it possible to pull a whole freight at once with four engines laboring together.

Despite the obstacles, the GNR announced, on November 11, 1909, "For 35 days the fastest long distance train in the world, from St. Paul to Seattle in 48 hours, has made good." The remarks, reported by the Wenatchee World, touted the GNR's new mail train, five cars only, which sped over the prairies and through the mountains in record time. The GNR was also operating speedy Oriental Limited passenger trains at this time.

During the operation of the Cascade Tunnel, there were humorous as well as tragic incidents. In a 1959 Seattle Times article, the GNR agent at Cascade Tunnel recalled that in 1911 the crew had been startled to see a man leading a cow emerging from the east portal. Upon querying him, the farmer replied that he had walked through the tunnel from Index, bound for Merritt, to save the $10 freight cost of shipping the cow. He was lucky, for the intermittent escape ports in the tunnel barely held a man, much less a cow, and think of the wreck if a train had come through while the cow was in the tunnel!

The GNR was able to solve its suffocation problem in the Cascades, but the avalanche problem continued. An ambitious program of snowshed construction ensued, mostly between Wellington and the Martin Creek trestle.

Still, in December 1907, the eastbound train left Skykomish in a blizzard, with drifting snow filling the cuts as fast as they were plowed. It took five hours to cover the twelve miles to Scenic, where the crew was reluctant to continue the nine miles to Wellington. The dispatcher insisted, however, and, preceded by a rotary snowplow, the train bore on. About two miles short of Wellington, an avalanche sealed off the entrance to a snowshed just cleared by the advancing snowplow. Separated now from the plow, the engineer quickly backed up into another snowshed, from which the train had just emerged. More slides roared down to close the train securely in the shed until it was unable to move in either direction. There it remained for ten days, at which time the crew and passengers walked out to Wellington. The train was dug out two days later.

Less than three years later, one of the world's worst railway disasters occurred. The action developed over a seven-day period, climaxing with a disastrous avalanche early in the morning of March 1, 1910. Three rotary snowplows and two GNR passenger trains, numbers 25 and 27, were involved. The two passenger trains had been detained at Leavenworth pending weather information. After some delay, the two trains went up the grade together on February 23 and were shunted onto sidings at Cascade Tunnel. It was then learned that a slide blocked the way to the west. Late the next day, the two trains moved through the tunnel and were parked on passing tracks beneath the town of Wellington. Rotary plows worked feverishly to free the tracks of snowslides, some with boulders and trees in them, but could not keep up, especially at Windy Point (about three miles west of Wellington), where slides repeatedly filled the tracks as quickly as they were plowed, finally reaching a depth impossible for the rotary to clear. The plow itself was being buried. Shovelers were called in from Wellington to help.

While Superintendent James H. O'Neill was everywhere at once, he and his crews were unable to keep ahead of the slides. The raging blizzard and heavy snow went on and on, day after day. As the largest rotary plow was returning to Wellington for coal, a slide 800 feet long and 35 feet deep came down between the plow and the train. Without fuel the plow was useless, and the trains now had no hope of getting off the mountain. Increasingly apprehensive passengers began to demand rescue and ask that the train be backed uphill into the Cascade Tunnel. Management negated that idea as too dangerous. Food was running low on the trains and in the town of Wellington itself. People were down to two meals daily of potatoes and bacon.

When O'Neill returned from directing slide removal west of the tunnel on February 26, the station agent told him that the telegraph line was out. There was no communication in either direction. The trains, plows, and people were totally alone in the wintry fastness of the Cascades.

On February 27, O'Neill and two brakemen, Jerry Wickham and J. S. Churchill, elected to walk to Scenic for help. Later that day, a party of five passengers set out, and on February 28 at least two other groups straggled out. John Rogers, one of those who made it to Scenic, described the situation prior to the avalanche in a March 4, 1910, *Wenatchee World* article:

At about 6 o'clock Wednesday morning we were stopped at the east

Twisted metal was all that remained after the Wellington avalanche. (Photo: North Central Washington Museum, Wenatchee, WA)

portal of the Cascade Tunnel. We stayed there until Friday, getting our meals, two a day, at a bunkhouse. On Friday night we left the east portal and a few hours later an avalanche wiped out the station and bunkhouse, killing two men. We pulled through the tunnel as far as Wellington, about a half-mile beyond the west portal.

At Wellington there are three tracks. On the track nearest the mountainside stood Superintendent O'Neill's private car, two boxcars, the engine and three of the electric motors used to haul trains through the tunnel. On these cars were the superintendent, train crews and porters. On the second track from the mountainside stood my train, consisting of engine, baggage car, two coaches, two sleepers and an observation car. On the third track stood the fast mail, on which were 16 or 18 mail clerks. About 16 track laborers were also sleeping on the train in the day coaches. We ate at Bailet's hotel in Wellington.

Sunday we noticed on top of this switchback [of the old route] far above us an enormous cap of snow hanging precariously on the side and clinging to the sparse timber. . . . That night there was a slide at the east portal which filled a 50-foot gulch. . . . The menace of that immense snow cap was a pall on our spirits. It was the most enormous accumulation of snow ever known in the mountains, according to the hotel keeper. During all this time it snowed continuously with terrific winds driving the drifts. . . . Monday night we decided we could wait no longer, and we set out to walk to Skykomish.

Another who trudged out reported to the Wenatchee World that his party crossed three immense slides, each about fifty feet deep, covering the telegraph poles entirely. Farther on, the men had to cut their way through a wrecked snowshed to go on. Finally, Scenic Hot Springs was in sight, but first they had to cross a giant slide, larger than the rest. "To linger meant death. To proceed did not hold much more," for the mountainside was almost vertical. The men could not walk; they could only slide down the mountainside, some 2,000 feet, at the speed of a toboggan. Some were injured, but all made it to Scenic.

Meanwhile, efforts at relief from Leavenworth were stalled, too, because a snowplow had cleared the tracks as far west as Chiwaukum, only to have more rock and snowslides come down behind it in the Tumwater Canyon. Now came rain, loosening the heavy snows barely clinging to the steep slope above Wellington—one that locals said had never before spawned a slide. Excerpts from the *Wenatchee World* (supplemented by the *Everett Herald*) best describe the developing crisis:

March 1. It is reported that a snowslide has covered the west-bound Spokane express, which has been stalled near Wellington. . . . Fear is expressed that some of the 30 passengers who remained with the stalled train have been killed.

[Meanwhile, crewman John Wentzel of Wellington made it to Scenic Hot Springs Hotel by daylight, gasping out the terrible news to Superintendent O'Neill, who was still in Scenic.]

March 2. Superintendent O'Neil [sic] of the Great Northern, directing the relief work in the mountains, telegraphs 60 lives lost yesterday in the avalanche. . . . From the east side of the Cascades the approach is cut off by a snowslide at Drury, six miles west of Leavenworth, which destroyed the station and killed Watchman Johnson. . . . The cars of the two Great Northern trains were carried 150 feet into the canyon and buried in the debris.

From the *Everett Herald*: A train left for the blockade scene of the Great Northern today with 70 additional workmen and supplies.

March 3. The disaster which overtook trains No. 25 and 27 at 4 o'clock a.m. Tuesday morning, March 1, grows more appalling. It is difficult to get positive definite information. . . . Without warning, the terrible slide overwhelmed the two trains, which were standing on the track below Wellington. The slide carried away the motor shed at Wellington and the four motors in it. It also carried away the coal chutes, water tank, and Superintendent O'Neil's car, killing Trainmaster Blackburn, Superintendent O'Neil's stenographer and cook. . . . One rotary at Windy [Point] was swept away completely by another slide which occurred later in the day and nothing can be seen of it. Two other rotaries were lost near the Martin Creek tunnel.

From the *Everett Herald*: Fifteen bodies were recovered from the snow heap of the avalanche . . . and there is no hope that any of the 69 persons missing are alive. One hundred and fifty men, mostly volunteers, are working to uncover the dead, but they can accomplish little owing to the huge mass of the debris which buries the cars. . . . The injured are at the Wellington bunkhouse and hospital. They have physicians, nurses, food and all comforts. All supplies are packed up the steep trail from Scenic on men's backs. The most pitied among the injured is Mrs. Wm. Starrett, of Chemainus, who is severely bruised. She was returning from Spokane, where her husband was killed in a railroad accident two months ago. With her were her three children, her father and mother. Two of the children and her father, William May, were killed in the avalanche.

March 4. Seattle's newspaper quoted. VICTIMS NOW REACH 118. . . . Of the dead 84 were passengers, trainmen and postal employees and the remainder were laborers. . . . In conveying the bodies down the mountain trail a toboggan made of boards and tarpalins is used. The bodies are laid on sleds, dragged over the snow, except in steep places, where men must lift the burden and carry it. Some of the bodies are mutilated but others are unmarked and have the expression on their faces of persons who never woke from sleep. . . . A mixed mass of snow, wreckage and gigantic trees whose trunks and branches are so interwoven with the other debris of the wreckage that it makes it impossible for men with no tools but shovels and axes to make rapid headway.

March 4. Bailets hotel, on the edge of the gorge, lurched toward the slope today and it is feared it will slide into the gorge [the clifflike cut where the railroad tracks were].

When contact was established, the few survivors of the trains swept into the canyon said the ride was like being on a storm-tossed ship. Adding to the unreality of the scene in winter, one passenger said in a March 4, 1910, *Wenatchee World* article, was the lightning:

> There was an electric storm raging at the time of the avalanche. Lightning flashes were vivid and a tearing wind was howling down the canyon. Suddenly there was a dull roar, and the sleeping men and women felt the passenger coaches lifted and borne along. When the coaches reached the steep declivity they were rolled nearly 1,000 feet and buried under 40 feet of snow.

One of the survivors was the train's conductor, Ira Clary, who was sleeping on train 27. Delwyn Nowak of Bellingham, Clary's nephew, says Clary found himself sitting next to a dead man. The conductor told a reporter that he had hit the top and bottom of the mail car several times in the descent. The car disintegrated after hitting a large tree. In a March 4, 1910 *Wenatchee World* article, Clary said, "When I realized anything I felt a sensation of suffocation and I found that I was buried six feet under the snow. I dug my way out." Clary and other survivors looked around, seeking to assist others. The steam locomotive had melted a big cavern where it lay, and Clary grabbed a companion to prevent him from falling onto the locomotive.

Charles Andrews, an engineer who had been sleeping in a little worker's cabin just before the avalanche, became uneasy about the growling of slides coming down in the area. Booming thunder followed brilliant bursts of lightning, a rare winter phenomenon. Andrews wandered down to the depot and then set out for the section men's bunkhouse, where a big stove gave out welcome warmth. His nocturnal prowling saved his life. Author Ruby El Hult interviewed Andrews around 1960, gaining a firsthand account of the disaster. Hearing a rumble, Andrews turned to see:

> White Death moving down the mountainside above the trains. Relentlessly it advanced, exploding, roaring, rumbling, grinding, snapping—a crescendo of sound that might have been the crashing of ten thousand freight trains. . . . It descended to the ledge where the side tracks lay, picked up cars and equipment as though they were so many snow-draped toys, and swallowing them up, disappeared like a white, broad monster into the ravine below.

With snow still blocking the railroad, bodies from the Wellington disaster were removed by sled to the nearest access point. (Photo: North Central Washington Museum, Wenatchee, WA)

When Andrews could make his feet move, he rushed to seek help, as Hult related: "Silent and as though moving in nightmare, he and the other men began to light railroad lanterns and button on coats for the descent into that valley of hell."

Volunteers from Leavenworth, Everett, and towns in between bravely battled the still-hazardous conditions to reach the site. As slide dangers eased a little, the GNR resorted to dynamiting through packed snow and ice slides to enable trains to reach Wellington. Rescuers began to remove bodies from the twisted wreckage.

Many of the injured were removed to Leavenworth because conditions on the east slope were better than those on the snow-choked western side. Nurses and doctors flocked to Wellington. Some of the injured were cared for there, and were able to move off the mountain themselves. Most of the dead were taken to Seattle and Everett.

Although no monetary value could be placed on the tragic loss of ninety-six lives (one body was not discovered until that following spring), the GNR estimated that the loss of track and equipment during the period was $2.5 million, more than half of that incurred at Wellington alone. The line was out of order for three weeks, costing millions more to the GNR and shippers.

The GNR was not alone in losing lives and equipment during that terrible winter: fifty workmen were killed on the Canadian Pacific Railway in British Columbia's Rogers Pass, and the Northern Pacific's routes suffered from the effects of the weather as well. But GNR's Wellington disaster went into the record books in 1910 as the third worst railway disaster ever. Indeed, the name Wellington evoked such horror in the minds of potential passengers thereafter that the GNR changed the name of the little town to Tye.

Already reeling and saddened by the tragic losses at Wellington, the GNR had to endure an inquest into causes of the event. After the hearings, the company was absolved of blame; the disaster was said to have been beyond human control. Later analysts have concluded that an obvious reason for the slides of the period was the denuding of the mountainsides adjacent to the track. It is theorized that construction personnel, many from the Midwest, did not fully realize the dangers caused by logging the slopes near the tracks. Other slopes had been denuded by fires set by sparks from locomotives laboring up the steep slopes, leaving marvelous opportunities for snowslides to develop during winter.

According to a December 15, 1910, *Engineering News* article, the GNR planned to complete the addition of 5,411 feet to the existing 7,593 feet of snowsheds (some of which dated back to 1893) by the forthcoming winter. The task included constructing 3,900 feet of rein-forced-concrete, double-track snowsheds at Tye, the site of the ava-lanche. In order to place these sheds in line with the contours of the mountainside, so that any future snowslide would continue smoothly over them, the double track was moved fifty to eighty feet north for about one mile. In 1913, almost three more miles of snowsheds were built, resulting in the coverage of more than 60 percent of the nine miles of track between Tye and Scenic. The railroad devoted as many as 2,500 workers to its battle for safety in the Cascades.

Before the GNR could enclose all its hazardous areas, however, fifty to sixty snow shovelers were killed in an avalanche 1,000 feet long and 200 feet deep on January 12, 1913. Most of the crew members were im-migrants—Japanese, Italians, Austrians, and a few Native Americans. Understandably, somewhat later the crews went on strike for higher wages to compensate them for the dangerous work.

At Berne, four and a half miles east of the tunnel and also a slide area, the tracks were moved from the south to the north side of Nason Creek for just over two miles. For drainage and fire fighting, small streams were led into barrels equipped with hydrants and hoses. Extra coal was stockpiled within the snowsheds to enable snowplows and trains to get free of the sheds if stalled for any length of time. The new snowsheds were successful in warding off most accidents during the 1913–14 winter.

Today's hikers along the Iron Goat Trail west of the old Cascade Tun-nel can marvel at the immensity of the materials used, especially the huge square timbers and the high concrete walls, many in sturdy condition, that once supported sheds.

Meanwhile, slide problems from both snow and rain-loosened rock were still occurring at the Tumwater Canyon section, northwest of Leavenworth. In 1916, W. J. Hoy & Co., a St. Paul contracting firm, set up three construction camps between Leavenworth and Drury, eight miles distant, to start work on snowsheds there.

Despite all the precautions that any human official could order, nature still overpowered the GNR on occasion: there were isolated train accidents and even another suffocation in Cascade Tunnel after the transmission lines failed. In January 1916, during one of the heaviest snowfalls on record (as much as one foot per hour), an avalanche swept a dining car and six day coaches off the tracks at Corea, near the east portal of Horseshoe Tunnel (west of Tye). A survivor of the dining car said snow poured in the windows like water; then the car rolled over and over and burned. Eight people died, and twenty or more were injured. Among the dead were Leavenworth resident Ed Batterman and his two small sons; his wife and another son survived.

Seeking to avoid a replay of the media circus that had surrounded the Wellington disaster, the GNR sent men to Corea to prevent newsreel cameramen from filming the scene. Instead, the cameramen—from the five major screen weeklies (Paramount, International Film Service, Animated, Pathe, and Mutual)—were hustled into an empty coach guarded at each end, and were kept there until a locomotive arrived to take them back to Skykomish, picture-less.

Snow difficulties continued right on through March of that year. The GNR had had enough. The idea of a long tunnel through the Cascades from Skykomish to Chiwaukum had been bandied about by citizens since at least 1910. As early as 1909, Army engineer General H. M. Chittenden had even suggested a thirty-two-mile tunnel to be built and used jointly by all the railroads of the Snoqualmie and Stevens Pass area, a concept reported in newspapers for many years thereafter.

The GNR had ideas and engineers of its own, however, and it set in motion plans to create a more reasonable eight-mile tunnel from Berne to Scenic, a passage still in use today. But construction did not begin until the mid-1920s because of the demands of World War I.

8. THE EIGHT-MILE TUNNEL

As early as 1914, after the snow problems of that period, James J. Hill himself had broached the topic of a larger tunnel through the Cascades. Preliminary surveys and a thorough analysis by E. J. Beard in 1917 called for elimination of the line through Tumwater Canyon and the construction of a new tunnel as long as 17 miles. However, the demands of World War I and labor shortages prevented action. In the early 1920s, further studies by engineer Frederick Mears showed that instead of the fourteen- to seventeen-mile tunnel suggested by Beard, a cost-effective 7.79-mile tunnel could be installed from Berne to Scenic, making it possible to retain use of most of the track on the east slope and between Scenic and Skykomish. In 1925, John F. Stevens was asked to give his opinion of the project as a consulting engineer. Stevens concurred with Mears's plan for a tunnel from Berne to Scenic.

While realigning the rails, the GNR decided to accept Beard's advice and eliminate the Tumwater Canyon portion, between Leavenworth and Merritt (another slide-prone area), replacing it with an easy grade northward through the Chumstick Valley, rejoining the old rails at Winton—today's Burlington Northern Railroad route. The GNR also planned to electrify the entire section from Wenatchee to Skykomish, thus avoiding the multiple changes of locomotives from steam to electric and vice versa. The Tumwater power plant's output was inadequate for such a project, so the plant was sold to Puget Sound Power & Light

One good reason for eliminating the Tumwater segment of the Great Northern Railroad was this snowslide and others like it. (Photo: Don Seabrook, The Wenatchee World)

Company (PSP&L) on March 24, 1926, with GNR gaining access to the larger grid of PSP&L's electrical system.

Puget Sound Power & Light Company served all of King, Chelan, and Snohomish counties until the latter two formed public utility districts and took over their own power generation in the late 1940s. A series of interlocking power lines serving Stevens Pass was called the Rock Island–Beverly Line, and GNR permitted PSP&L to number its poles as the utility's poles, in order to avoid confusion. Stevens Pass was known as a "hazard area" because the line had to be patrolled on foot, skis, or snowshoes to ascertain that it was not "down" in the often stormy weather. A patrol cabin near Yodelin was used to store supplies and as a shelter for patrolmen caught in bad conditions. The company had a private high-line telephone system with phone shelters built at intervals, so that trouble reports could be called in promptly.

The process of locating the 7.79-mile tunnel began in December 1925. Essentially, transit lines of ten-mile increments were "laid" to place a precise line over the top of the mountains, somewhat like heaving a line over a rooftop. When the transit work was completed, refinement of the axis was made possible by mounting a high-powered telescopic instrument, a theodolite, to adjust minutely the lines from Berne to Big Chief to Cowboy and down to Scenic, plus some intermediate monuments. Even though it took years for the men working from either end to reach the center of the tunnel, the survey was so accurate that when they did meet, the error of closure of the main tunnel was only nine inches on line and three inches on grade.

The GNR allowed only three years for construction of the tunnel, making several working faces within the mountain necessary. The shallowest earth above the tunnel was in the Mill Creek valley, so an 8-by-24-foot shaft, 622 feet deep, provided access to the "floor" of the tunnel. Here the surveyors also installed accurate, if primitive by today's standards, surveying equipment to enable excavators to follow the axis line laid out from Berne to Scenic: two piano wires, nineteen feet apart and resting on crosspieces, were suspended from reels down the shaft, to which were attached two sixty-pound plumb bobs in tubs of water to minimize their movement. To ascertain that the wires hung straight, a transit at the surface was monitored. At the bottom of the shaft, two transits were installed on opposite sides of the plumb line and aligned exactly with the wires. Through expert monitoring of this surveying equipment, an exact parallel line could be maintained, enabling workers to excavate a straight path almost eight miles through the heart of a mountain range.

A. B. Guthrie & Company gained the construction contract for the tunnel work. To provide entry to the projected subterranean site and to subsequent working faces, the builders used a method successfully employed for the Simplon Tunnel through the Swiss Alps and later for the Connaught Tunnel of British Columbia—a "pioneer" tunnel parallel to the main tunnel, much smaller and used for access, removal of debris, laying of ventilation and electrical conduits, and other necessary tasks. The pioneer tunnel was eight feet high and nine feet wide, driven both ways from the Mill Creek shaft (stepped over sixty-six feet). When completed, a small mining-style railroad ran through the pioneer tunnel. Every 1,500 feet, a crosscut over to the main tunnel, of precise length to line up with the axis, opened up additional working spaces and also enabled water in the main tunnel to drain. If copious amounts of water were intercepted, the workers could retreat until it drained, as there was an overall grade from east to west of 1.565 percent. Piping shunted persistent water along the side of the pioneer tunnel and outside, and sumps were dug to collect water at the Mill Creek shaft, with pumps moving the collected water up and out to the creek. As many as eleven faces were eventually worked simultaneously.

Meanwhile, on the surface, camps with all basic amenities were built for the crews and families. At the peak of construction, 1,700 men were at work somewhere along the tunnel's length. The buildings, including service buildings such as mechanic shops and storage sheds, were built on stilts six to ten feet above the ground to minimize the problems of snow removal in winter. Each camp had changing houses called "drys," where men could come to the surface, damp and cold, get a hot shower, and change into dry clothes. The camps had running water and electricity, and the cookhouses had refrigeration equipment. There was a recreation building for such activities as card playing, reading, and regularly scheduled movies. Near the married employees' quarters there was an elementary school. A hospital with a resident physician guaranteed early care to injured or sick employees and their families. The buildings were lined up along a boardwalk "street," with boardwalk entries to each dwelling. Sanitary waste was collected in septic tanks. There were camps at Berne, Scenic, and Mill Creek. A few workers may have commuted from Tye, Skykomish, or elsewhere, as records show board allowances for those crewmen living at home.

Guthrie's crews were professional and dedicated. They were further motivated to do fast, efficient work by Guthrie's offer of a footage bonus

Workmen and a mule emerge from the pioneer tunnel, a smaller access tunnel adjacent to the main one. (Photo: Special Collections Division, University of Washington Libraries, neg. Pickett 1816)

plus their hourly wage and the opportunity to set a world's record for speed in completion of the tunnel. On their own, the crews at the various headings developed an intense rivalry as to which working face could move forward the fastest. According to Frederick C. Bauhof in *Engineering Geology in Washington*:

> The camp with the best excavation record for the month flew a "high camp" pennant from the flagpole for the next month. The pennant had on it a Rocky Mountain goat design, the emblem of the Great Northern, and it created the desire to "get the other camp's goat."

Here are some examples of the pay scale, which represented top wages in 1926: underground laborer, 60 cents an hour; driller, 80 cents an hour; electrician, 80 cents an hour; cookhouse waitress, $45 a month and board; truck driver, $100 and board; general foreman, $250 and board; master mechanic, $300 and board. Employees were normally charged $1.35 per day for room and board, and men living at home and commuting were given a board allowance of $25 a month.

Close attention to time management contributed to the speed of the work, with crew changes made at the various sites, not outside the portals. Three eight-hour shifts were maintained all day, every day.

Since preliminary surveys showed that most of the tunnel went through solid rock, there were few problems with bracing or cave-ins. A drill carriage held four compressed air drills that hammered away simultaneously at the rock to create blasting holes. Workmen retreated into the pioneer tunnel during the actual blast and then surged forward to "muck out" debris from the ever-larger main tunnel. Along all but the major portals of the tunnel, small track-mounted Myers-Whaley mucking machines loaded the fifty-cubic-foot dump cars. The cars were on a scaled-down rail system that operated through the pioneer tunnel and through most of the crosscuts, using just twenty-four-gauge rails. Six-ton electric locomotives moved the little trains out to the open air, using electricity provided by an overhead trolley. One battery-operated locomotive was always kept in reserve for rescue work in case anything happened to the electricity. Most of the debris was good granite rock and was utilized for roadbed fill beyond both ends of the tunnel. The GNR was straightening its lines as much as possible as part of the overall project.

At the major portals, removal went much faster, with air-driven power shovels used to remove debris to dump cars, which were pulled by larger, twenty-ton electric locomotives on thirty-six-gauge track.

Workmen excavating the pioneer tunnel set a world's record during one month, moving 1,157 feet. In the main tunnel a "cycle" of excavation was established that averaged 7.6 feet forward for the entire

Workmen waiting to enter the tunnel; shift change occurred right at the work site. (Photo: Special Collections Division, University of Washington Libraries, neg. Pickett 3865)

circumference of the tunnel, and took an average of four hours and forty minutes with a crew of sixteen men. A cycle consisted of the following procedure: blast, wait twenty-seven minutes to ventilate blast area, enter and remove debris, set drill carriage and drill holes, load with dynamite and retire to safety, then blast again. Excavations in the main tunnel included specified refuge bays with telephones every 1,200 feet.

The rounded, domelike ceiling of the tunnels left room for the attachment of the overhead trolley system. This was a standard catenary construction with an 11,000-volt stranded copper messenger cable attached every seventy-five feet by a three-unit suspension type insulator with a voltage rating of 60,000. A single copper contact wire (to bring power to the train) hung from the messenger cable. To maintain absolute tunnel alignment, the surveyors worked from a platform suspended above the action below, a surveyor using a transit there to line up exactly with the transits outside the portal. Within the mountain, workers excavated from readings obtained in the parallel pioneer tunnel until breakthrough enabled them to make line-of-sight readings to either portal or the precise plumb-bob rig in the Mill Creek shaft. From these readings, with precise measurements through the crosscuts to the main tunnel, exact positioning of the main tunnel could be achieved. When the pioneer tunnel came together on May 1, 1928, the error of closure was only .64 foot on line, .78 foot on grade, and 1.9 feet on distance.

The tunnel was faced with concrete as soon as it reached the specified proportions—sixteen feet wide and twenty-five to twenty-seven and a half feet above subgrade. This was to prevent rockfalls in subsequent years. Since the site where the concrete was applied could be as much as four miles from the outside, it was impractical to mix the stuff outside and move it in. Instead, a concrete system was hauled to the site of application, and aggregate was sent in as needed. The "jumbo" car carried the concrete mixer, hopper, distributing chutes, conveyor, and pneumatic concrete gun. Standard chutes directed the concrete to the lower portions of walls, and for domes or difficult higher points, concrete was inserted into steel forms with the concrete gun, a bit like squeezing grout into tile.

An automatic signal system was installed. The technology was updated as more sophisticated systems evolved, but the original system called for light signals bolted onto the tunnel wall (red for stop and green

A huge shovel is nevertheless dwarfed by the earth it is excavating. (Photo: Special Collections Division, University of Washington Libraries, neg. Pickett 3676)

for proceed, with some three-color units for indicating stop, proceed, and caution). The system included positive and redundant controls beyond each portal to assure that no slips could occur that would allow trains to collide within the tunnel. Electric lights were staggered every seventy-five feet throughout the tunnel.

A rail bed of washed-gravel ballast was laid twenty-one inches thick. Tracklayers installed seven-by-nine-inch creosoted ties eight and a half feet long, then 110-pound rails. When the easterly and westerly tunnel bores came together, the "holing through" was triggered by President Calvin Coolidge, who pushed a remote-control button in the White House.

While there were line changes on the west side, particularly on a segment of new track between the west portal and the original track near Scenic, the major change was on the east side. Unfortunately for Leavenworth, the new Chumstick Valley route also skirted the city and further curtailed the business that the town had gleaned from GNR activities. The Tumwater Canyon segment was abandoned. After June 11, 1929, the town was served only by a Dinky, one train each way daily. The further downscaling of the town's importance, which had begun with its loss of GNR headquarters status in 1922, was a severe blow to Leavenworth's economy.

The Chumstick Valley route took off from Peshastin, three miles below Leavenworth, to angle over to the northwest side of the valley. About eight miles north of Leavenworth, the line curved back west through a 2,601-foot tunnel and later a 4,059-foot tunnel to join the original line near Winton and proceed toward Stevens Pass. A smaller Swede Tunnel lay between the two. The new routing, still used today, was able to maintain shallow curves no greater than three degrees (the original had nine-degree turns) and an easy grade. The first train over the new Chumstick route was the mail train of October 7, 1928, which left Peshastin at 12:42 A.M. (the Eight-Mile Tunnel portion was not yet open at this time).

The tunnel was completed on December 24, 1928, and the Chumstick Valley revision connected the through tracks less than a week before the formal opening ceremonies on January 12, 1929.

The opening was indeed newsworthy. NBC aired the event over a hookup of thirty-six radio stations. At the east portal, NBC's Graham McNamee introduced Ralph Budd, president of the GNR, who dedicated the tunnel to James J. Hill. Additional speeches were given by J. B. Campbell of the Interstate Commerce Commission and General W. W. Attebury of Pennsylvania Railroad. Opera star Ernestine

The GNR's first Oriental Limited entered the Eight-Mile Tunnel on January 12, 1929. A festive crowd cheered the tunnel's completion. (Photo: North Central Washington Museum, Wenatchee, WA)

Schumann-Heink sang a song on radio remote, NBC's McNamee described the trip through the tunnel from the west portal, and President Herbert Hoover gave a speech from Washington, D.C.

A special train, filled with media people and dignitaries, was set to travel through the tunnel from east to west. It was pulled by one of the GNR's spanking-new electric locomotives and pushed by another. But instead of proceeding through the tunnel, it halted at the east portal, stalled out from condensation caused by the change in temperature at the mouth of the tunnel (it was warmer on the west side). The pusher could not move the train alone. While a third locomotive frantically moved into position to assist, thirty-five minutes went by. At the west portal, waiting broadcasters ad-libbed until they ran out of topics, then filled in with band music. To everyone's relief, the special train finally burst through the paper covering the west portal. At 7:00 P.M. the dignitaries met at a banquet in Scenic at A. B. Guthrie's camp. Here there were many more speeches by luminaries including engineers John F. Stevens and Colonel Frederick Mears, Washington Governor Roland H. Hartley, and GNR board chairman Louis Hill, Jr.

The GNR continued to update its long tunnel as conditions warranted. Because the system was electrified from Skykomish to Wenatchee, high-capacity ventilation methods were not required. The GNR began to use diesel engines as helpers in 1944, when trains became heavier and the crossings slower. The catenary system was beginning to need repairs or replacement. Since diesel locomotives were replacing steam and electric trains nationwide, it again became necessary to modify the Cascade Tunnel (by this time, "Cascade Tunnel" meant the Eight-Mile Tunnel, not the old Cascade Tunnel). In 1954, the International Engineering Company was engaged to design a ventilation system, and the Morrison-Knudson Company was contracted to build it at the east portal in Berne.

The resulting system, still being used today, is curious. As an eastbound train lumbers up the ascending grade into the tunnel, a door at the east portal closes and one huge fan blows cool air into the tunnel, over the laboring diesels. The intrusion of the train into the tunnel acts much like a piston in a casing. After the entire train has cleared, the door closes and two fans purge the fumes from the tunnel for thirty minutes. No train may enter the tunnel during that period. Even though westbound trains are coasting downhill, the tunnel is purged behind them, too. Amtrak passenger trains are so light that they do not require ventilation in either direction. In 1990 another necessary change was completed: reaming out notches in the overhead dome to accommodate the new double-stack container trains.

The new Cascade Tunnel eliminated most of the avalanche problems and many of the dangerous curves of the prior system. It is the longest railroad tunnel in the United States and the second longest in North America, outdistanced only by the 9.11-mile tunnel through Rogers Pass in British Columbia.

LEAVENWORTH

9. TOWN BEGINNINGS

The building of the Great Northern Railroad was the catalyst for the development of a sprinkling of villages, settlements that began as construction camps, and at least three fair-sized towns along Stevens Pass—Index and Skykomish, at the western end of GNR's Cascade Division (see Chapter 13), and Leavenworth, at the eastern end.

As discussed in earlier chapters, the populating of the area today called Leavenworth began with the Wenatchi Indians and the settlers who moved to the area from Icicle to be near the GNR tracks. A land development firm, the Okanogan Investment Company, laid out a new town in 1892, naming it Leavenworth after one of the four chief investors, Captain C. F. Leavenworth. J. P. Graves apparently continued as an active financier, but two of the original investors, Samuel T. Arthur and Alonzo Murphy of Spokane, sold their holdings to Captain Leavenworth in 1893.

Leavenworth had been active in many other Northwest ventures. The *Washington Standard* credited him with building the Olympic & Gray's Harbor Electric Company railroad in 1888, the large Cosmopolis Mill & Trading Company sawmill, and a mill near Port Townsend. He was appointed in 1891 by the lieutenant governor of Washington to begin plans for the University of Washington.

The GNR proceeded to swiftly clear the forestlands and build a depot, a roundhouse, and bunkers. Workers and merchants moved in.

By February 1893, about 700 people populated Leavenworth. Forty or fifty business houses opened: stores selling dry goods, groceries, shoes, and drugs, as well as restaurants, hotels, and saloons. In 1900, Anne Tholin Reeves was Leavenworth's only female shopkeeper; after graduating from high school, the young entrepreneur opened The Sweet Shop, later adding stationery and gifts to her wares. Major A. S. Lindsay published the *Leavenworth Journal* until 1898, then left town. Deed H. Mayar started the *Leavenworth Echo* on January 15, 1904.

To furnish lumber for homes, businesses, and railroad ties, the Woods Brothers lumber mill, which had been logging along the Wenatchee River farther east, moved to Leavenworth and employed about seventy-five men. (Years later, Woods Brothers was operating near Skykomish.) The town grew so rapidly that an addition was platted on April 1, 1893, by the Leavenworth Real Estate and Improvement Company.

To provide medical care for railroad personnel and others in 1893, the GNR sent Dr. G. W. Hoxsey to practice in Leavenworth. He became one of the town's most beloved residents, a legendary country doctor who would even snowshoe to serve his scattered patients during winter. The GNR set aside a small cemetery just east of the entrance to Tumwater Canyon, and provided free interment for its deceased employees there. A pleasant plot with a picket fence, it is shown in certain photos of the area taken in the early 1930s. By 1966, only three headstones remained, marking the graves of children who died in 1893, 1894, and 1904. Stan Herald, the present-day owner of the property, offered to donate land in 1966 to restore the small cemetery, but no action was taken on his offer. Leavenworth residents have worked sporadically to clean up the brush-filled locale, in the process uncovering other markers. In 1992, there were five markers, but all the old headstones have vanished from the site.

On March 12, 1899, the state legislature passed a bill forming the new county of Chelan from parts of Kittitas and Okanogan counties, its boundaries the same as today. Governor John R. Rogers made it official by issuing a proclamation on December 7, 1899; a May 1900 census put the new county's population at 776. Wenatchee became the county seat.

Turn-of-the-century timber magnates were looking to the West for new forests to conquer. Chancy Lamb, a mill operator since the mid-1800s in Clinton, Iowa, sent his son Lafayette to purchase several fine stands along Nason Creek toward Stevens Pass at prices reportedly as low as $10 an acre. Lamb-Davis Lumber Company (LDLC) incorporated for $250,000 in 1903 with Lafayette Lamb as president and Petrel Davis (also of Clinton) as co-partner, treasurer, and general manager. The company built a mill in Leavenworth, entering the lumber business in earnest and creating a payroll of $25,000 a month within two years. The firm also built a boardinghouse for employees and a small company hospital, managed by Dr. William McCoy. The company bought all the remaining lots of Leavenworth's original town site. They acquired the local water company and built an electric plant, making the town one of the first in the state to enjoy electric lights.

LDLC built a dam across the Wenatchee River, below today's hospital, to act as a storage pond for logs. In memoirs at the Leavenworth Ranger Station, James Fromm, a pile driver for LDLC in 1907, recalled that he and other lads rode peeled cedar logs down the river into the millpond as a lark. The small dam could be opened to release water when log storage was not required.

To preserve the local Indians' ability to do subsistence fishing, LDLC set aside 400 feet of riverbank above and below the dam for their use. The Indians came during salmon season in buggies and on horseback to catch and dry their seasonal supply.

Leavenworth became an incorporated town on July 28, 1906, with

Leavenworth in 1919 (Photo: North Central Washington Museum, Wenatchee, WA)

Echo publisher Deed Mayar elected mayor. At that time Leavenworth had a population of 1,000, largely supported by the mill and railroad but including a few miners.

Leavenworth remained a teeming industrial center for a quarter century. As a mill town and headquarters of the Cascade Division of the Great Northern Railroad (in 1905 renamed the Great Northern *Railway*), Leavenworth could not be called quiet. Every weekend it was the target of workers bent on assuaging their weekday loneliness by drinking, fighting, and womanizing. The buildings were crude, the streets virtual cattle tracks. Household water was carried in barrels from the river. Since there were no bridges across the Wenatchee River, which was usually too deep to ford conveniently, residents bound for Ellensburg or Wenatchee traveled along the north bank of the river to the Peshastin ferry.

Fire was to plague Leavenworth town for the first decades of its existence. The first blaze, in 1894, burned out Bill James's barbershop and T. C. Owen's jewelry store. The next conflagration, in 1896, destroyed an entire block of the business district (curiously, the same block the 1894 fire had incinerated), including the Overland Hotel (owned by John Bjork), Bisbee & Donahoe's Saloon, Posey's barbershop, Severton's Saloon, a restaurant owned by Mrs. H. A. Anderson, J. M. Duffy's Saloon, and the home of one Mr. Belvel. Six years later, in January 1902, the town burned again. This time the losers were G. C. Merriam's general store, Mrs. Beamish's millinery shop (housed in a building owned by G. C. Christensen), and J. W. Poag's restaurant and confectionery.

Fire struck Leavenworth again on January 24, 1904, destroying six buildings. GNR employees were assigned to help fight the fire, and local residents pitched in. Nonetheless, gale-force winds drove the fire from Adams & Burke's poolroom, where it started, to Plisch & Bliss's store, which it consumed. L. W. Bloom's meat market, opened only three weeks earlier, was another loser, as was the Overland Hotel (again), The American Hotel restaurant and lodging house, and Walker & Company's saloon. Other merchants lugged their stock onto the streets, away from buildings, only to have thieves make off with much of it in the darkness.

On June 7 and 10, 1904, two more blazes visited Leavenworth. On a windless night, the first burned only a livery stable and home. But only sixty hours later came a far more destructive fire, causing significant or total loss to Leavenworth Mercantile Company's warehouse (where the fire started), City Drug Store, Tholin & Smith's saloon and lodging rooms, Tumwater Cafe, Greeve's barbershop, and barns and residences. The beloved Dr. Hoxsey lost expensive instruments and his

precious library; attorney L. J. Nelson, in the same building, was simi-
larly hard hit.

Heroic efforts by townspeople saved the rest of the town, but the
post office was scorched and Tumwater Savings Bank's windows were
blown out. The *Echo*'s building was damaged, but not by fire. According to an *Echo* account of June 10, 1904:

> To prevent the fire spreading to the *Echo* office and the adjoining
> Merriam buildings across the street from the Cascade, three attempts were
> made to blow up the hotel. The first two with powder and the third with
> dynamite. Nearly a hundred sticks of dynamite were placed in the rear end
> of the Cascade hotel. It exploded with a deafening roar and sent lumber,
> beams and debris flying in every direction. All the doors and windows in
> the front end of the *Echo* office were literally smashed into splinters, and
> the building considerably shaken up. This, though, no doubt helped to save
> the office.

Undaunted by the fire losses, Tholin & Smith opened a rather grand
opera house on December 13, 1904, with a minstrel show and "burnt
cork" rendition (apparently a spoof) of *The Mikado* by the Wenatchee
Dramatic Club. The *Echo* reported, "The jokes at the expense of the
democratic party, burlesque dialogues and grotesque situations, were sand-
wiched between songs, choruses and dancing. Mr. Jas. Duff's character-
ization of Kadesha provoked much fun." The invitational opening of the
Opera House Bar two weeks earlier featured a barbecued-pig dinner with
hors d'oeuvres of crab and shrimp, no doubt imported from Seattle on
the GNR. Later programs included such performers as The Great
McEwen, a hypnotist; and Lee Willard, a comedian. The Scenic Theater also opened, giving townspeople another source of entertainment.

Lest one believe that Leavenworth was getting too civilized, though,
in June 1907 in the Opera Bar, an intoxicated lumber worker named W.
L. Davis shot fellow patron John McGee point-blank just because
McGee kept slapping Davis on the back. When a railroad detective in
the bar tried to restrain Davis, the lumber worker turned the weapon
on the officer and pulled the trigger twice, but the gun was empty. While
patrons talked heatedly of lynching Davis, police hustled him out of town
on the next train to Wenatchee's jail. The next morning Davis was said
to be prostrate with grief, remembering nothing of the night before.
Formally scheduled fights at the Opera House included an April 1908
bout between Denver Ed Clark and Kid Raymond.

The Opera House building still stands in Leavenworth, housing city
offices on the first floor and the city's library on the second. (The first
floor originally housed the Opera Bar; the auditorium and stage were
on the second floor.) To support the weight of the expected crowds, the

The Lamb-Davis Lumber Company and its successor, the Great Northern Lumber Company, were major Leavenworth area employers. (Photo: North Central Washington Museum, Wenatchee, WA)

builders used joists three inches thick and twenty inches wide, with sixteen-inch spacing. Walls were eighteen inches thick, and there were no posts or pillars to obstruct views of the raised stage. The interior was paneled with cherrywood. Still drawing admiration are the graceful brick arches accenting each window of the building.

Among the expanding businesses in 1906 was the two-story Losekamp Building, which housed Losekamp General Store, the Tumwater Savings Bank (owned by the LDLC mill), a hotel, and two meeting halls. Other enterprises included J. W. Elliott's saloon, restaurant, and lodging house; King Company's general-merchandise store; Hathaway & Swank's three-story saloon and lodging house; John Bjork's hotel; Emil Frank's meat market (which had a hall overhead); and the Congregational Church. A new financial institution, the Leavenworth State Bank, was formed by a group from North Dakota and Iowa led by Robert B. Field and including C. J. Weiser, E. J. Weiser, S. M. Lockerby, and Fred A. Sinclair.

At this point LDLC had a daily capacity of 100,000 to 120,000 board feet of lumber and 20,000 to 25,000 board feet of lath; its box factory consumed an additional 30,000 board feet of lumber. A total of 300 men were employed in the mill and the logging operation. Increasing numbers of fruit orchards were being planted in the area; as they matured, shippers required boxes to ship their crops, helping LDLC's business. Downriver from Leavenworth, a mill opened at Peshastin. It was said that a logger could down a tree in the morning, sell it to the mill for $4 per 1,000 board feet, and the tree would be made up into apple boxes by nightfall.

Another industry on the march was sheep raising. With grazing rights on the newly established national forestlands, sheepmen trailed their sheep into the valley from the more-arid lands across the Columbia River. In November 1907, statistics showed 35,000 sheep in the Mount Stuart area, 25,000 in Icicle, and 6,500 around the White River of the upper Wenatchee Valley. Sheepherders faced hazards other than high-country snow, loneliness, and straying of sheep. In 1908, a Portuguese sheepherder made the mistake of shooting one bear cub and wounding another in the upper Wenatchee Valley, whereupon the understandably irate sow attacked him, tore off the flesh of his jaw left great scratches across his eyes, took off his lower lip, and bit his leg. Only the intervention of his dog saved the man's life.

In May 1906, Leavenworth citizens petitioned the GNR for an overpass of its downtown tracks, which were used by about twenty-five locomotives each day. Residents were concerned about the peril to schoolchildren and about the several accidents and near-accidents that had occurred. A horseback rider died when his horse refused to leave the track. Another died crossing the tracks on a bicycle.

The citizens' petition was granted; a high wooden overpass over the dangerous midtown tracks was built that year, with the GNR paying the construction costs and the town promising to pay for maintenance. The overpass had to be rebuilt in September 1909, however, after a spectacular wreck demolished it. During switching operations, a car jumped the track and smacked into the bridge supports. The force of the train behind it compounded the problem by forcing the car against a coal car, lifting it in the air and flinging the stock car on top of the coal. The whole mess continued on into the space below the viaduct, but by then it was too tall and further wrecked the structure so that it fell on top of the train.

The local mill, Kelley & Lapp, was purchased in 1909 by S. B. Hathaway, but it was LDLC that dominated the timber business at that time. Logs were taken not only from the Nason Creek area but also from the heavy forests of the upper Wenatchee Valley. The company itself owned 50,000 acres of timberland. Much of the actual logging was performed by Adams & Costello, which built substantial camps and barns for its crews and teams in remote areas.

Big logs were cut on the White and Wenatchee rivers during fall and winter and were stacked in huge piles unti the spring runoff. Loggers dynamited the piles to roll them into the rivers. A crew of river-drivers then followed the logs downstream all the way to the mills. In and out of the river, unable to carry spare clothing, workers were half wet all the time, day and night, but most thought the trip a great lark.

If the logs were above Lake Wenatchee, they came down into that broad body of water to be boomed and towed to the foot of the lake. Shingle bolts were processed at the small mill there, and booms of larger logs were dismantled to continue their trip down the Wenatchee River to the LDLC mill at Leavenworth. Camp F, a logging camp between Fish Lake and Lake Wenatchee, dumped logs into the lake as well. Residents of Plain, too, worked logs from their area down into the Wenatchee River.

W. O. Burgess, as tough and colorful as his pioneer father W. W., one of the first settlers of Plain (see Chapter 3), was working loose a tangled mess of logs in the river after a dynamiting when a shore worker accidentally set off a further charge, sending another batch of logs down on top of W. O. Although he was thought to be lost for a while, he had actually been shoved clear under the log mass and so had escaped being pulverized by the second set of logs. Half-drowned in the process, he managed to stay alive until the shouts of fellow loggers alerted the shore crew to stop the log flow. He crawled out unscathed, in what seemed like a miracle to those who thought he had surely perished.

W. O. and the Dickinson boys, members of another pioneer family, were among the river-drivers riding the logs to Leavenworth. They alternately piked the logs hung up on shore or rode the logs downriver as if they were bucking broncs. In Tumwater Canyon, where the river quickens into seething rapids, the logs often got hung up in the rocks. Log drivers casually walked out on the heaving mass of logs with dynamite in their pockets, lit a fuse, and returned to shore before they "blew."

In 1907, LDLC created the Wenatchee Valley & Northern Railroad (WVNR) to transport logs from forest to mill. Originally the railroad was also envisioned as a means for tapping the Red Mountain mining area, where several promising digs had opened. George McDonald became superintendent of the new railroad and, under his direction, logging of the right-of-way to the head of the Chumstick River was completed that same year.

Only two years later, twenty miles of the WVNR were in place; ten miles more would be completed, although the railroad was so crooked that it was dubbed the Peavine Railroad. But it did the job. It was also said

A typical logging train hauled huge logs over incredibly steep grades. (Photo: Special Collections Division, University of Washington Libraries, neg. Pickett 1247)

that the WVNR used more lumber to build high trestles than it took out of the woods. At slack times the WVNR hosted sightseeing trips. According to the *Wenatchee World*, 100 Wenatchee Commercial Club members boarded the train on May 18, 1910, for the trip up the Chumstick. The flatcars had seats but no roofs; when the wind blew passengers' hats off, the engineer accommodatingly stopped the train to retrieve them. Club members declared the scenery the equal of that in Switzerland.

By 1912, LDLC had seventeen logging camps in the area, producing 50 million board feet of lumber daily. About 500 men were housed in camps scattered from Leavenworth to Plain and Lake Wenatchee—those of LDLC, Adams & Costello, and other smaller independents. The company had a double-band sawmill with a daily capacity of 215,000 board feet, a planing mill, a box factory, and management buildings.

The tensions of running LDLC seemed to be too much for F. J. Kline, its manager in 1913—possibly the firm already had financial difficulties. One day when F. C. Riggs of the Tumwater Savings Bank came to his office, Kline was there. He warned Riggs that if he came in, Kline would shoot him. Riggs did not take this seriously and walked in, whereupon Kline did put a bullet into Riggs's shoulder. Kline made his point: Riggs, suffering only a painful flesh wound, left precipitously. Kline's action was laid to temporary insanity.

After financial difficulties in 1915, the firm closed for a year. In January 1917, the entire holdings of LDLC, including timber estimated to yield 650 million board feet, were sold to the Great Northern Lumber Company (GNLC). (Despite the name, this firm was not associated with the GNR.) It was capitalized for $1.65 million; the president was Frederick T. Boles of Chicago, and other officers came from the Midwest, too. George Gardner was its first superintendent, succeeded by F. S. Seritsmeier of Portland in 1919.

The GNLC ran a decent operation, maintaining clean camps for its crews. Most "camps" were railcars parked on a siding, easily moved as logging progressed. The beds were clean, the food good. Logging was beginning to attract a different kind of man, one more likely to spend his off-duty money on movies or ice cream than to soak himself in whiskey.

Methods of logging were changing too, taking advantage of advancing technology. The company built spurs up Freund Canyon, Spromberg Canyon, and Eagle Creek to access company-owned tracts. Gone were the ox or horse teams that used to drag the logs out; instead, donkey engines and cable brought logs to the rails, to central yarding points for transport, or to riverside for floating to Chumstick River. As logs in the valley were depleted and logging moved into higher country, the logs were manhandled to the edge of a steep hill to be shoved onto special skidways or flumes that brought the logs to the railroads. The GNLC had a holding pond at Chiwaukum, from which it released logs to hurtle downstream to Leavenworth when the water was high enough.

High was hardly the right word in late May 1921, when flooding caused pilings to give way at the Chiwaukum loading works, sending 18 to 20 million board feet of logs down the river. For a time it was feared that the fugitive logs would take out the lumber company's dam and do other damage, but the logs just kept on going, winding up on Wenatchee River shores all the way to the Columbia.

When the 1920s brought practical logging trucks onto the scene, the company began to add them to their fleet for transporting logs to the rails or directly to the mill. As trucks became ever more practical and forests adjacent to rails depleted, the company's railroad—which never did come close to the Red Mountain mining area—ceased to operate in 1927.

While the GNR was building its original rail line and then the Cascade Tunnel, a host of other small mills sprang up to satisfy the railroad's need for lumber. Most closed after the railroad was completed. Sam Beecher built a sawmill on Mountain Home in 1905. Leavenworth Lumber Company was incorporated in November 1912; owned by F. S. Jacobson (later a banker), it produced boxes for the fruit industry. There were shingle mills as well. The C.A.C. Shingle Mill at the foot of Lake Wenatchee, owned by W. J. Detrline, began operation in 1936, shipping its shingles from Winton; it was later sold to H. Kielbaugh and William "Buster" Hermann. Young men cut cedar into seven- and eight-foot lengths, tied them into booms, and dragged them off to the mill by boat for processing into shakes and shingles. By nature, logging and mill work was dangerous. Men were sometimes trapped under booms and drowned, their bodies showing up downstream. In one case, a log jumped out of a chute and killed a logger who was sitting nearby whittling.

C. A. Harris and son Arden started a mill in 1914 at Winton to make ties for the GNLC, operating as a branch for the company. At Peshastin a box mill thrived, fueling a small town of about two hundred where the train slowed only to pick up the mail sack suspended from a pole beside the track.

The GNLC operated profitably until the late 1920s, at which time price reductions that were a forerunner of the Great Depression caused financial problems. The stockholders chose to close the company before it was too late. Added to the 1922 departure of the GNR headquarters at Leavenworth, the closure was a body blow for the town.

To take up the slack in lumber supplies, the Nason Creek Mill Company began operations four years later, in 1931. It was incorporated by H. J. Merz, Leonard Wunder, and Martin Christenson. All were experienced lumbermen, Merz having been GNLC's superintendent, Wunder a GNLC employee, and Christenson a private mill owner. Its early cuts were sold to Peshastin Saw Mill & Box Factory to satisfy the insatiable need for fruit boxes by the Peshastin Fruit Growers Association.

As Leavenworth expanded, so did speculation about putting a trail or wagon road through toward Seattle. In March 1907, a bill creating the Icicle-Kittitas Road was passed and signed by Washington's governor. Money was appropriated for the survey and building of a road from Leavenworth up the Icicle River Canyon, to cross at some point to Snoqualmie Pass. One estimate put the cost of construction to Kittitas County at about $13,500. Supporters pointed to the mining discoveries in the Icicle area as a potential source of revenue for the county and state. In a May 24, 1907, Echo article, Al Van Epps and Bob McGough, miners in the mountains above Icicle, said they came and went from Seattle via Cle Elum, in Kittitas County.

Nothing came of this proposal, except the eventual construction of a road up Icicle Canyon, giving hikers access to the Alpine Lakes Wilderness Area. Icicle Canyon did become the site of a remarkable irrigation project, however, a forty-mile ditch that stretched from ten miles up the Icicle River to the town of Monitor, fifteen miles east of Leavenworth.

E. E. Hall and C. E. Chase surveyed the project in 1904, but it was not until 1910, after a more comprehensive survey, that construction commenced. Capitalized for only $10,000, the Icicle Canal Company was formed. The chief promoter was W. T. Clark, builder of Wenatchee's High Line Canal. One of the incorporators, L. P. Horton, was also the superintendent of the job, with Fred M. Berry, Chelan County engineer, assisting with the planning. (His son, Lloyd G. Berry, later became manager of the Icicle Irrigation District.) Sixty men with shovels and horse teams, nails, and hammers energetically went to work building ditches and flumes. Tapping into the Icicle, the flumes were virtually hung on the sides of the mountains, supported by trestle-like structures as they descended. About a mile and a half from Leavenworth, the canal split into two parts—one veering north to serve the lower Icicle Valley and on through Leavenworth to the Kinscherf tracts north of the city, the other continuing on down to water the valley's orchards as far as Monitor.

The water at that time came strictly from the Snow Creek area, emanating from Snow Lake into the Icicle. In order to regulate and not waste the irrigation water, engineers designed a curious contrivance that, in lay terms, acted like a drain plug to Snow Lake. The "plug" was opened when water was needed and closed after sufficient flow was attained.

The original canal effort was underfinanced, unfortunately, and the $2.50-per-acre assessment for the approximately 25,000 acres having water rights was insufficient to keep the Icicle Canal Company afloat. It went bankrupt and into receivership in 1912. The state took over the company and sold bonds to finance the operation, assuring orchardists of water. By 1917, the entire system of canals and flumes was in dire need of updating. The Icicle Irrigation District was organized, with J. E. Griffith as the first secretary. Much of the capital came from local orchardists, but—with the urging of Walter M. Olive of Cashmere, the promoter of the project—C. H. Black of the Seattle Hardware Company agreed to furnish construction money in return for acquisition of several hundred acres of heretofore arid lands. After the canal was completed, Black recouped his investment by reselling the land with water rights. The directors assessed users $7 an acre, and there were 4,000 irrigated acres. The irrigation district then sold bonds to supplement the direct income. Claude Zediker was in charge of replacing faulty wooden flumes with concrete ones. Crews using dynamite and teams of horses with scrapers dismantled one section of old flume at a time and rebuilt it, so there would be little interruption of service.

To control the flow of water, a patrolman or ditch walker traveled the flume to open and close gates to siphons or U-shaped supply canals leading to those landowners possessing water rights. The present Chelan County engineer, Lloyd Berry, was occasionally drafted by his engineer grandfather to run up to Snow Lake to close the outlet or walk the ditch line.

Irrigation-ditch operation was not without danger, because of the considerable current in the ditch. During spring, the irrigation district started operation early so orchardists could spray for insects. Sometimes ice floes plugged up the ditch. One year a floe jammed in the Pine Flats tunnel, and while Claude Zediker and Jake Chriswell were clearing the jam, they were washed down the canal for a considerable distance. They stayed afloat in the water-and-mud mixture by holding onto their shovels and had to be dug out of the "soup" by other crewmen. On another occasion, Zediker was pulled under the ice while he attempted to clear a jam. Another worker ran downstream and stuck his shovel into a hole; Zediker grabbed it and pulled himself to safety.

The system made possible the burgeoning growth of the fruit industry in the otherwise arid valley, bolstering the economies of Leavenworth and the lesser towns downriver and creating a need for boxes as well as farm and shipping supplies.

Today the irrigation ditch is still flowing, and it still must be treated with respect. The control method still exists, with more sophisticated additions, and the system now draws water from Klonaqua, Colchuck, and Square lakes as well as Snow Lake.

10. BOOMTOWN

By 1910, Leavenworth's future as a regional rail, mining, and lumber center looked bright. The mines at Red Mountain hinted of major development. The Mount Stewart Mining Company began mining asbestos on Ingalls and Allen creeks. The rich Blewett mining district also benefited the town. There seemed to be no end to the verdant timber; Adams & Costello alone was bringing in logs that resulted in 20 million board feet of lumber at the mills. Appleton & Carter planned to open a shingle mill on Lake Wenatchee. A company called Alaska Marble discovered a large deposit of marble on Chikamin Creek, twenty-eight miles from Leavenworth toward Red Mountain. (Production lagged because of financing problems for several years, however.) There was talk of building an electric railway to link the towns from Wenatchee to Leavenworth. Hyman Harris of Wenatchee received a franchise to construct an electric railway from Leavenworth to Colockum (in the Ellensburg area), although nothing ever came of it. The Icicle Canal was being built. Land around Leavenworth was selling for $100 to $500 an acre.

One enterprise that sparked excitement ultimately fizzled. There were rumors of an iron and steel plant in 1907. In June 1911, Washington Steel & Iron Company did let a construction contract, planning for two buildings and a spur from the main Great Northern Railway line. By December that year one of the buildings was completed, and steel rolling equipment, other heavy equipment, and an ore conveyor were in place. On February 7, 1913, the *Leavenworth Echo* reported an order of six tons of steel from a company in Leeds, England. The Leavenworth firm soon doubled its output, obtaining some of the raw materials from a body of magnetite eight or nine miles from town.

The company was headed by E. H. Rothert, who said he had a secret process by which the magnetite of the area could be converted to steel. Unfortunately, two years later local stockholders were demanding to know why Rothert was not manufacturing more steel. Although Rothert defended his process and had turned out small batches of steel, the stockholders petitioned for a receiver for the factory, the process, and other property. Rothert obtained an injunction to prevent the directors from acquiring the formula from a safe-deposit box at the Traders National Bank in Spokane, where it reposed in a sealed envelope. The resultant litigation was settled in 1915, with Rothert retaining his secrets and some property but surrendering the bulk of the Leavenworth operation to stockholders. The factory was dismantled and sold, as was the equipment, ending Leavenworth's dreams of becoming a steel center. Rothert set up a small furnace near his home, where he insisted his process was workable. Whether the man was an inventive genius, a crackpot, or an entrepreneur who had worked some sort of stock scam, no one seems to know.

Another curious Leavenworth enterprise was the warehousing of ice. In 1913, the GNR shipped ice taken from its annual ice harvest in Marion Lake, Montana, to Leavenworth for storage—up to 225 carloads of it.

In addition, toward the end of 1913, it was announced that a major state fish hatchery would be established at Leavenworth, on land donated by J. B. Adams. Construction began in early May 1914 under the supervision of E. E. Sherwood. When completed, the facility consisted of a hatchery measuring twenty-eight by sixty-five feet, including a small office, and a dwelling twenty-six by forty-four feet, occupied by the first superintendent, Henry Baldridge. Traps were set in the river to catch spawn for the following year's crop of fry. The hatchery was capable of managing up to 2 million fry at its inception. In 1919, it hosted 1.5 million fry, all scheduled for release that year into Chelan County streams—500,000 steelhead plus trout, mostly cutthroat. As time went by, Eastern brook trout that had been planted in streams were to be "milked" for spawn, and Snow Lake and Twin Lakes in the Icicle drainage were reserved for spawning purposes. Three million fry were released with the volunteer assistance of Chelan County sportsmen in 1923. (This hatchery, successful though it was, would be overshadowed in another fifteen years by a huge hatchery installation at the junction of the Icicle and Wenatchee rivers.)

The generally good economic picture prompted pioneer merchant F. A. Losekamp to remodel his building to include a hotel. Other prominent businesses included the Mutual Mercantile Company, Tumwater Savings Bank (backed partially by the GNR), and the Chikamin Hotel. The Barclay Building, three stories of brick, went up in 1913. Wenatchee Meat Market and The Golden Rule opened, and the City Drug Store was sold. The apparent prosperity attracted thugs, too. In July 1913, safecrackers using nitroglycerin attempted to rob the Leavenworth Lumber Company. A logger assaulted a police officer, grabbing the marshal by the throat, but the officer "played a regular tattoo" on the culprit's head, according to the *Echo*.

In the boom environment, a fledgling industry that would eventually support the area—tourism—was being born. Tourism depended on convenient transportation, and the automobile was rapidly becoming a practical means of traveling from the population centers west of the Cascades into the mountains. On the west side were the tattered remains of the old tote road of the 1890s, really just a trail that had been pushed forward to move freight to the GNR railroad camps. This first road in the Skykomish Valley was hacked out of the forest; traffic soon turned the trail to miserable mud in many places. It was so narrow that sometimes wagon wheels would scrape trees on both sides. If teams and wagons sank out of sight in the mud, crews threw in more cedar logs to alleviate the situation. During the winter, crews shoveled out the road, working mostly at night so traffic could proceed by day. The narrow road also facilitated the exploration of the upper valley by potential settlers; on traveling the tote road, passengers usually abandoned the wagon and walked, unable to endure the awful jolting over puncheon road—puncheon being logs laid side by side crosswise in boggy places, nearly unbearable for anyone with a bad back.

Yet it was a start. Businessmen eyed the GNR's abandoned switchbacks as a possible part of a new scenic highway. In 1911, L. H. Titchenal of Cashmere first envisioned the road as a wagon road (although he said auto enthusiasts were interested in a road over the pass, too) because there already was a road as far as Merritt. Only ten more miles to connect the road to the switchbacks would be required, at a cost he estimated at $15,000. The idea caught fire. Some, including Chelan County engineer Fred M. Berry at first, negated the idea of a Stevens Pass route, favoring improvement of the Blewett–Snoqualmie Pass road. After a trip over the switchback route with Will White, engineer of the highway commission, Berry estimated that about forty-five miles of road would have to be built—all the way from Merritt to Index—at a cost to the three counties involved (King, Snohomish, and Chelan) of at least $200,000. He then threw his support behind the Stevens Pass route, although he pointed out the advantages of connecting Leavenworth with Ellensburg via Blewett. Wenatchee booster Percy Scheble favored the switchback route to Tye, saying that only twelve miles of new road would have to be built to connect with an existing road (his "road" was a "trail," though). Newspapers tossed around the figure of $1,000 a mile for forty-five miles. Berry, the professional engineer, proved more correct in the long run, but he too was low in his cost estimates.

In May 1912, residents between the Snohomish County line and Scenic organized a Good Roads Club to promote a cross-Cascades highway. The group, under Millard Fillmore Smith of Berlin, secured an appropriation from King County for work as far as Skykomish. Two months later, a booster group called the Scenic Highway Association was formed in Everett, with George Startup of Startup as president, L. H. Titchenal of Cashmere as vice president, and W. W. Baird of Everett as secretary-treasurer. Trustees came from eastern and western Washington. A group of decorated automobiles entered a Seattle parade during July to promote the road.

On a bright Sunday, July 28, 1912, boosters from the east side took the train to Cascade Tunnel, then hiked along the switchbacks to meet west-siders west of Tye. Engineer Berry made the hike and announced that the switchback route was feasible. He reported that the switchback grades were in astonishingly good condition, considering their age and disuse. A week later, a Snohomish group made a trip via the old Cady Pass route to compare its possibilities with that of Stevens Pass. Two weeks later another party was in Stevens Pass to view matters firsthand, this group composed mostly of Seattle and Everett residents but also including reporters from the *Everett Herald*, the *Seattle Post-Intelligencer*, and the *Seattle Times*.

At a Good Roads Club meeting in Wenatchee on August 24, 1912, a surprise visitor was Louis W. Hill, chairman of the GNR's board, who volunteered his company's complete cooperation. He raised a thorny problem, though, of the ownership of the switchbacks. The Northern Pacific had originally received land grants to construct a railroad through Stevens Pass. Using private capital, the GNR had built without grants and over some of the Northern Pacific lands, including the land underlying the Cascade Tunnel. Hill conjectured that the switchbacks and other lands would come under an "abandoned highway" classification and would revert to the federal government. As it turned out, ownership rights were not a serious problem, and plans went forward.

Matters moved fast. Engineer Berry did survey the Stevens Pass route more closely. All in all, twenty-eight miles had to be built in King County, twelve in Chelan, and seven in Snohomish to create a through road. In November 1912, King County passed an appropriation of $165,000 to build its portion; it was then up to the other two counties to make good. Fred Berry estimated that Chelan County's portion—a dirt road, no highway surfacing—could be completed for $45,000. In a January 3, 1913, *Echo* article, he expressed excitement over the project: "Here is a roadway [switchbacks] which has lain for 12 years without any repair whatever and it is to-day in excellent shape. I don't believe there is another approach for a road to the Cascade mountains which could be constructed for as little money as this one."

In March 1913, a Leavenworth chapter of the Good Roads Association was organized, led by F. L. Brender, J. E. Gutherless, and F. S. Jacobsen.

Snohomish County reportedly planned to do $30,000 worth of work on the road. Chelan County had not made an appropriation by March 1913, so H. B. Smith, the Merritt Hotel owner, started a petition for private donations. Citizens chipped in with sums from $5 to $100. King County representatives came to the east side and threatened to delay work until Chelan County could assure construction of its share. Contractors Quigg & Scaman did some work on the highway in late 1916, but the east side was incomplete. While Chelan County dragged its feet, apparently lacking the funds, King County essentially finished its section by 1917. The U.S. Forest Service donated $90,000 toward the road, backing it as a means of expanding access to the timberlands for fire fighting and public recreation. Chelan County's work was completed from Leavenworth to Merritt; then progress was stalled because of the cost of building two underpasses of the railroad, a bridge, and some remaining road between Berne and the tunnel. A road supervisor named Parish suggested that citizens should think about rerouting the road up Tumwater Canyon, which was more scenic and fifteen miles shorter to boot.

But the road, limping along for lack of highway appropriations from all three counties, went untraveled. The distractions of World War I made tourism unimportant. In April 1917, eight soldiers were assigned to Leavenworth to guard the roundhouse, the GNR's dam, the Cascade Tunnel, and other points. Ninety-two others were stationed at key rail points (including bridges) from Berlin to Odessa. They warned that anyone who failed to respond when challenged would be shot.

With so many men away at war, Leavenworth's business houses closed in late October 1917 to free every able-bodied person to harvest the apple crop. The lumber mills ran at top capacity, supplying lumber and boxes for crops and military purposes. Because of the lack of male workers, fifteen women went to work at the Great Northern Lumber Company mill in September 1918, a first for the area.

Fruit growing continued to forge ahead, creating a stable market for sawmills and box companies. The market tightened when the Peshastin Lumber Company was leveled by fire in August 1919. The firm immediately rebuilt; after all, one orchardist alone, H. G. Bohlke, needed 100,000 boxes—and there were hundreds more growers in the area.

The lumber company wasn't the only business in the area that burned down during this period. Leavenworth's many wooden structures made it particularly susceptible to fire. On May 31, 1914, a fire that started in a home at the rear of the Lobby saloon spread to consume the tavern, N. B. Day's confectionery, the Clifford Hotel, Morimoto's rooming house, and other structures. The proprietor of the saloon saved his liquor; he had built a concrete storage area beneath the saloon that extended beneath the town's sidewalk. Four other blazes followed, three or four weeks apart, leading authorities to suspect an arsonist at work. The blazes destroyed the Hub clothing store, a livery barn, two blacksmith shops, the Roach harness and shoe store, the Seeley tin shop, and other structures. Later in 1914 the entire Bjork block burned, destroying what was left of the Lobby saloon, the Overland Hotel along with a bar and restaurant, and the Windmill Pool Room. Before the year was out, the post office building burned as well, taking several other businesses with it. Several businessmen pooled their capital and built the Leavenworth Brick Factory to produce bricks for rebuilding. The lasting quality of brick construction is evident in the sturdy buildings of Leavenworth today.

Irene Gordon, the proprietor of the Overland Hotel, may have been having second thoughts about city life after having been burned out yet again. In September 1914, she purchased the Lake Wenatchee Club House on the lake. Earlier the popular resort had operated as Dirtyface Lodge, a private club for key people and guests of Lamb-Davis Lumber Company. By 1928, Gordon had sold the popular resort to the W. B. Patons. It was a delightful lodge of massive fir and pine logs, 145 feet long and 60 feet wide, with porches on three sides. A spacious lounge and dining room with three huge stone fireplaces gave charm and warmth to the large rooms. Dancing and variety programs entertained the guests. There were rooms in the main lodge, plus furnished cabins and tents. Mrs. Paton was noted for her wonderful meals, but guests could cook in their cabins if they wished. Visitors enjoyed fishing, hunting, horseback rides, and just cozy days next to the fireplace in fall.

Like other boom towns, Leavenworth wrestled with vice problems. Back in 1908, a big flap developed over the July Irrigation Congress celebration, which was highly touted and attended by many Wenatchee Valley residents. Before the night was over, visitors were complaining about drunkenness, lack of accommodations, and being overcharged for hotel rooms. As a July 6 *Wenatchee World* editorial put it, "It took three hours to pull off three horse races. A dinky confectionery stand sold lemonade in dirty glasses for ten cents a glass." The *World* blamed the chaos on "the lack of effort on the part of the business men of Leavenworth to do anything to help matters." Stung by the criticism, the city fathers voted to close taverns on Sunday at least, and talked of opening a reading and recreation room so tavern devotees would have some place to go. The moral indignation gradually drained away, though, and tavern life continued to coexist uneasily with family values.

Burglary and holdups at gunpoint were not rare in Leavenworth. At one point the police discovered a thriving gambling house; featuring poker, blackjack, moonshine liquor, and sake, it was favored by Japanese laborers. Thirty-one participants were arrested and paid $2,691 in fines. Respectable taverns and pool halls such as The Club catered to the restless males of the area, but imbibers often came to blows. The strangest local crime was the attempted murder of two orchardist families; an unknown person pumped poison gas into their houses. A quarrel over water rights in 1917 caused J. W. Coon to shoot Mr. and Mrs. Joseph Charlton, his neighbors.

Leavenworth was no worse than other frontier towns, of course; it just had a flammable mixture of semitransient laborers, railroad workers, and loggers. The town, which had grown to about 3,000 by this time, did have upright families as well as toughs, however, and it staged cultural events of astonishing variety and excellence. There was an annual six-day Chautauqua featuring readings, science lectures, concerts with such luminaries as the New York City Concert Quartet, dramatic productions such as *Shepherd of the Hills* with a New York cast—a real culture binge. "Smokers" for men were popular—usually boxing and wrestling matches.

During the summer of 1925, the Famous Players–Lasky Corporation, producers for Paramount Pictures, shot the movie *The Ancient Highway* at Lake Wenatchee and Leavenworth. The stars of the movie, Jack Holt and Billie Dove, and the host of supporting players and crew attracted gawkers from beyond the town. Local people, including loggers from the Great Northern Lumber Company and Rider Lumber Company, were employed as extras. Loggers from the latter company staged a realistic fight for the cameras. The November 20, 1925, *Echo* reported that "this fight contains more than the ordinary amount of thrills for the movie fans . . . a few of the participants . . . found in this movie fight an opportunity to lawfully settle some long standing grudges."

For one scene Jack Holt, in train garb, became the engineer on a GNR Oriental Limited train ascending toward Stevens Pass and monitored by Leavenworth's real engineer, L. E. Gant. A staged flight by Billie Dove across the Wenatchee River on logs to rescue her lover almost became a tragedy when Dove fell in and under the logs. GNLC extras plunged into the water to save her, but she extricated herself. All in all, Wenatchee Valley residents had a grand time during the two months of filming.

A sobering event shocked Leavenworth in 1922: the GNR decided to move its headquarters to Wenatchee. Gone were the town's hopes for a new roundhouse and new depots, along with the prestige of being a GNR center. For a time Leavenworth did not hurt too much, however. Lumbering was still booming, and the fish hatchery was expanding to release more and more thousands of hatchlings into streams for tourists.

Ah, tourists. To develop a tourism industry, a Stevens Pass road was still needed. In February 1922 hotel owner H. B. Smith renewed his lobbying. The USFS was to spend $1.3 million on road work, and Smith believed that half of that work would be within the forest reserves. The USFS indeed did spend more money on the Stevens Pass road, and other county appropriations were received as well.

While Stevens Pass Scenic Highway was under construction, highway workers were among the many patrons of Smith's small resort along the highway above Merritt. Smith had operated the Merritt Hotel until it was destroyed by fire on July 21, 1913. The timing was unfortunate, for Smith, a strong supporter of the effort to build Stevens Pass Scenic Highway, had already helped to raise $5,000 to build four miles of road toward the pass and had hoped his hotel would eventually benefit from automobile tourism. Smith and his wife, Ellen, moved up the highway, to a place closer to Stevens Pass. They put in a gas station and authentic log cabins and named the small resort Rayrock Springs (after their son Raymond).

Smith's son, Raymond "Cascade," played his own part in the development of the Stevens Pass area. He obtained an engineering degree from the University of Washington in 1925 and designed the overpass at Stevens Pass and two small airports. He was a specialist at bridge design; in fact, he was offered a partnership by Morrison-Knudson but refused, according to his daughter, Ramona Dudek. He also worked on the Eight-Mile Tunnel.

Stevens Pass Scenic Highway apparently had traffic prior to its official opening in July 1925; this photo is dated June 17, 1924. (Photo: Special Collections Division, University of Washington Libraries, neg. Pickett 3908)

Wenatchee resident Dudek, who stayed at Rayrock Springs frequently, is full of stories about her grandfather, H. B. Smith, and his resort. She notes that he was quite a promoter:

> We had a silica mine, actually just a big boulder. When grandfather would rub two pieces together, it sparked, so he set up a stand to sell pieces to tourists. Then he built a water fountain that came over the rock as a waterfall. He painted the rock white and made a sign, "Ponce de Leon Looked for It and Here It Is—The Fountain of Youth," so everyone stopped to get water.

Dudek remembers sitting on that rock the day of the World War II armistice, waving a flag at the tourists. Smith named the cabins after his granddaughters and furnished them with Dutch beds. Dudek recalls a couple who went to look at one of the cabins at the start of the season, and found a bear inside. "The man beat the woman back to the car," she laughs. (Ramona and her sisters, on the other hand, had a pet bear who loved cola.)

In the winter, snow completely covered the cabins. The main resort was popular with skiers, of course. It was a fixture until the 1980s. Raymond Smith eventually retired in Wenatchee, and the family leased out the lodge to various people over the years. One night in 1985, an overflow group stayed in Smith's house, which had been vacant for some time, and accidentally burned it down, destroying antique skis, snowshoes, and bearskins. Some of the resort buildings, however, can still be glimpsed along the westbound division of today's highway.

Back in 1924, the day finally arrived when headlines blazed: "1st Auto Over Stevens Pass on Saturday, Nov. 1." That first auto's trip was hardly routine sightseeing, though. A Mr. Collins of the Pacific Overland Company drove a car to Everett (from Seattle, presumably), where he was joined by Abe Glassberg of the *Everett Herald* and another intrepid passenger, Bailey Hilton. The three headed eastward on October 31 at 5:00 A.M. until they arrived at Alpine, the end of the "passable highway." There the auto was drawn by cable up a logging incline to the Alpine mill. It then bumped along behind a freight train on the railroad ties, over frighteningly high trestles, through claustrophobic tunnels and snowsheds, the passengers fainting from fumes, to Tye. Only Collins and Hilton experienced this part of the journey; Glassberg quite sensibly refused and walked from Scenic to Tye on the partially completed new road. On November 1 at 8:00 A.M., twenty-seven hours after their departure from Everett, the three determined travelers struggled to the summit with two of the men on foot part of the time, pushing the car through snow and mud. Near the summit, a contractor took pity on them and used his team to pull the car over the top. They threaded down the switchbacks under their own power. Meanwhile, at Tye, a telegram was sent to the Leavenworth boosters, who started up to Cascade Tunnel over a fairly good road to rejoice with the west-siders, arriving at 12:30 P.M. All four cars then descended to Leavenworth, and the first crossing was history.

After supporters realized that a cross-mountain highway could not be maintained properly with a hodgepodge of county appropriations, the Stevens Pass Highway Boosters club was organized at a dinner in Sultan on May 15, 1925. Its purpose was to encourage the state to take over the scenic highway as a primary state highway. The group elected officers and adopted resolutions.

Stevens Pass Scenic Highway opened officially on July 11, 1925. An estimated 1,200 people in 283 cars turned out to dedicate the road at the pass; it was the second cross-mountain road in the state (the Blewett-Snoqualmie road was first). On the beautiful summer day, picnic baskets came out of the cars.

A *Wenatchee World* reporter driving to the opening ceremonies got lost while heading westbound, as he attempted to sort out the various roads around Merritt; then he got a flat tire. He camped out for the night and eventually made it to the summit the day after the opening. In his report for the *World*, he raved about the beauty of the area, the coyotes serenading him while camping, and the new red and white gas station on the highway.

George Startup, as master of ceremonies, called on Governor Roland Hartley, county commissioners, state highway engineer J. W. Hoover, Snohomish National Forest Supervisor W. C. Wieger, Mr. and Mrs. Frank Havens (pioneers of the pass), and others. Governor Hartley introduced Peggy Green of Monroe as queen of Stevens Pass. Also in attendance was Wenatchee National Forest Supervisor A. H. Sylvester, who had cooperated vigorously with booster groups in working for the highway.

The road was designated primary state highway 15 in 1937 and US 2 in 1948. In 1963 the state of Washington designated it SR 2 to bring it into compliance with the federal signage and numbering system.

Jake Beattiger was the first commercial business operator at the summit of Stevens Pass. (Photo: Don Seabrook, The Wenatchee World)

11. SKI TOWN

The 1920s and 1930s saw keen interaction between transportation and recreation in the work of the Great Northern Railway, the U.S. Forest Service, and the Stevens Pass Scenic Highway promoters. As described in Chapter 10, Stevens Pass Scenic Highway opened to traffic in 1925, though it was little more than a narrow, sometimes graveled road. Immediately thereafter, lobbying efforts began by those seeking to turn the road into a major highway under state or federal auspices. The USFS was involved because tourists increasingly used the road, as bad as it was, to access the forests. The GNR's route changes resulting from the construction of the Eight-Mile Tunnel also affected the Stevens Pass road location.

The USFS was very involved in preparing the forests for an expected boom in campers and hikers. F. W. Cleator of the Portland USFS office came to Stevens Pass and pointed out that although the work of platting and mapping the government lands at the pass was finished, there were few facilities for campers. Berry pickers were taking thousands of gallons of huckleberries from the area opened up during switchback construction in the 1890s. In response to the demand for overnight facilities, the USFS had developed a few forest campsites, but because the number of sites was insufficient, overflow crowds were building campfires along the switchbacks. Cleator predicted that it would be necessary to encourage commercial development of the pass to serve visitors.

In 1924, the USFS pinpointed three necessary recreation-related developments: a gas station and store at Scenic; commercial development and a forest camp at the summit; and a resort, campground, and tavern at Mill Creek. That same year Jake F. Beattiger constructed a service station and store for a total cost of $755. In 1929, he added two cabins; in 1931, a power plant on the Tye River; and between 1931 and 1937, a water system for his own use. The collection of small structures known as Beattiger's Resort was moved from the south to the north side of the road during 1935–36 to make way for expansion of the Stevens Pass highway, and Beattiger acquired two cabins from Puget Sound Power & Light to use as additional rentals. In 1950, Beattiger built the Summit Inn and operated it until it burned in 1969. The old store and gas station were demolished in the early 1970s.

A letter from George Flanagan, recreation foreman for the Stevens Pass area, to Cleator on January 3, 1934, recommended the expansion of camping facilities, stating that berry pickers often stayed for several weeks, sanitation was poor, and a water system was needed.

Before World War I, skiing as a sport hardly existed in the Northwest. In fact, when Olive Rand of The Mountaineers showed up on a 1912 tour of Mount Rainier with skis, she was received dubiously—deservedly so, for her skis were mere slabs of wood with turned-up ends; loops over regular boots kept them on, after a fashion. Other Mountaineers spent much time on that tour rescuing Rand from some predicament or other, as the wobbly skis went their own ways.

During World War I the government trained elite ski troops to operate in the European mountains. Among the corps were Washingtonians who looked for places to ski after they returned home. At that time there were no lodges, no lifts. Further, skis were very long, boots were made of leather that soon admitted melted snow, and the bindings were no more reliable than Rand's 1912 version.

Around 1930, Paul Scea, John Parkhill, and Walker Pickens of Wenatchee trekked to Stevens Pass and searched for a ski lodge site, but nothing came of the idea for some time. Mountain downhill skiing as we know it today was relatively rare; skiers slid down their hometown hills or went cross-country.

It was in Leavenworth that skiing took off, during the time when ski jumping became very popular all over the West. In 1926, Walter Anderson of the USFS and Milt Cloke were the key promoters of a ski hill for Leavenworth. It was constructed at the northern outskirts of town, on what is today Ski Hill Road. Volunteers worked on both a skiway and a toboggan slide. The Great Northern Lumber Company donated lumber for the ski-jump trestle.

A ski jumper waits to start his run at a Leavenworth ski hill. (Photo: Special Collections Division, University of Washington Libraries, neg. Pickett 4692)

With the help of the USFS and an army of volunteers, the official Leavenworth Ski and Toboggan Course was in operation by the winter of 1928–29. Leavenworth's hill, built for just $300 cash plus hours of volunteer labor, was said to compare favorably with the best courses in the nation—courses that cost twenty times as much. The hill was 375 feet high from the top to the bottom of the landing slope, as tall as a thirty-story building. Its slope was more than 53 percent, so steep that workers had to pack the snow to keep it from sliding off. Another 700 feet constituted the "runoff." A 240-foot trestle extended from the take-off point toward the starting point, crossing a deep ravine in the hillside. The supporting poles varied from sixteen to thirty-two feet and were dragged up the hill by men and tractors.

On one Sunday in early January 1929, the *Leavenworth Echo* reported, 500 people were using the course. Only a few dared to tackle the "big ski course," but many tried the amateur jumping course. February 10, 1929, marked the first Leavenworth winter-sports tournament, with more than 1,000 people attending. The expert jumpers invited included Segurd Hansen of Ione, Washington, who had won the world's championship in 1913; Walter Anderson of Leavenworth; and S. A. Anderson and Vic Anderson of Cle Elum. Hansen won a silver urn for his soaring jump.

By the 1929–30 season, the course had gained fame among regional jumpers. The Pacific Northwest Championship Tournament on February 23, 1930, attracted twenty-nine skiers (eleven failed to qualify) for the Class A competition, some from Seattle; Vancouver, B.C.; and Revelstoke, B.C. Two hundred spectators came on a special Great Northern Railway train from Seattle and Everett, swelling the audience to perhaps 3,500 people. Nels Nelson of Revelstoke won the event.

Leavenworth's hill was deemed to be one of the finest in the Northwest circuit, and the field expanded each year. In 1932, Norwegian jumper Nordahl Kaldahl of Vancouver, B.C., jumped 126 feet to break the local record. Then local legend Hermod Bakke appeared; it was his first time in Class A competition. He came in sixth but would soon sweep away all comers.

In 1933, the fifth annual tournament, held in ideal skiing weather, was won by Tom Mobraaten of Vancouver, B.C., who jumped 183 and 192 feet. During an earlier practice, John Elvrum of Portland, deemed the most spectacular jumper in the West, soared 210 feet and 201 feet but fell in competition, as did local star Bakke, who jumped 186 feet. But the work of the newly organized Leavenworth Winter Sports Club was gratifying, with 4,000 spectators crowding the tourist facilities from Leavenworth to Wenatchee. There was speculation that the hill one day might be judged a worthy site for the Olympic Games. Following the jump competition there was a big dance at the Odd Fellows' hall that was packed with so many swaying couples that one reporter said the hall developed an accordion motion.

In the 1934 meet, Hermod Bakke came in fourth out of a large field of jumpers, with 5,000 spectators in attendance. The following year a still-increasing audience watched Bakke jump 201 and 200 feet to win the tournament and the right to represent the association at the Olympic trials in Salt Lake City. It was the first time that the Pacific Northwest Ski Association had won the right to send a skier to the trials. The locals were exuberant; the February 15, 1935, *Echo* reported, "Bakke was in great form and on his own hill he was invincible. The biggest skier of them all—180 pounds of nerve and daring—he was out to put on a show for the huge crowd, and twice he flew through the air with the greatest of ease." A month later Bakke won second place at a big Portland competition. He did not make the Olympic team in 1935, but he went on to be crowned Pacific Northwest champion in 1936. There were skiers at Leavenworth from Norway, Japan, and Eastern Europe, among them Birger Ruud of Norway, Bakke remembered.

Bakke and his brother Magnus were born in Hurum in eastern Norway. As youngsters there, they competed in four-kilometer cross-country races. Both men worked for the USFS out of Leavenworth. Magnus was a forest guard and trail builder, responsible for laying out some of the ski trails at Mission Ridge south of Leavenworth. Hermod was a lookout at Lake Wenatchee's David site and at Rock Mountain on Stevens Pass.

Jumping skis of the 1930s were eight feet long and made of hickory, Hermod Bakke recalled. His longest jump was a whopping 255 feet, but that was in practice only. He said he was never hurt during his jumping career, although once he jumped with a cracked rib and another time with a sprained ankle. He observed:

> Skiing has quite a bit to do with balance. You needed strong legs to sort of launch yourself. You were supposed to land with one foot ahead of the other. It was quite a thrill. The Class A ranking was based on form, technique and achievement.

Huge crowds attended the ski meets at Leavenworth, which became a site for major competitions. (Photo: Special Collections Division, University of Washington Libraries, neg. Pickett 4693-A)

The lanky man made his last jump at age fifty-eight in 1960, but he continued to ski for pleasure until 1978. In December 1971, both Hermod and Magnus Bakke were inducted into the National Ski Hall of Fame at Ishpeming, Michigan, for their service as well as for their skiing.

The ski meets continued to draw large crowds, an important economic boost that carried Leavenworth's merchants safely through the Depression era. Under the leadership of Magnus Bakke, a ski hut was completed in 1935–36, the "hut" being a one-and-a-half-story hillside lodge that the USFS built of rock from Hatchery Creek and rustic logs. In the main warming room, a nine-foot fireplace could accommodate six-foot logs to warm the ski crowds. The lodge also included a small lunchroom and caretaker's quarters.

Leavenworth's fame continued to grow, making its name familiar nationally. In 1936, Leavenworth's Helge Sather jumped 242 feet, breaking the national amateur record by ten feet, but he fell on landing, as did Bakke, who injured his ankle when he fell on a leap of 233 feet. Six weeks later, however, Sather was crowned Pacific Northwest champion for Class A combined cross-country and jumping.

The 1937 tournament attracted 1,800 people by train alone; three special runs were made from Seattle and Everett. The *Echo* reported on February 12, 1937:

> With 44 passenger cars parked on the Great Northern tracks in town Leavenworth had all the appearance of a bustling railroad center Sunday and the puffing locomotives moving cars at the yards added to that appearance. . . . More than 1500 requests for reservations had to be turned down by the Great Northern because of lack of cars.

In fact, that year the GNR had to borrow cars from the Northern Pacific and the Milwaukee Railroad. In addition to the 1,500 people left behind in Seattle, the newspaper report asserted that the Weyerhaeuser Company had planned to schedule a tournament outing for all 3,600 of its employees, but the GNR was unable to provide the cars. Leavenworth was truly living up to its growing reputation. In 1938, Ken Binns of the *Seattle Times* wrote that Leavenworth at tournament time was crammed so full of people that "when you try to eat, you may be taking someone else's ham sandwich."

Spectators cheered their favorite skiers and groaned when they fell. They argued about which were the best natural skiers—those of Austrian or Norwegian descent. The ayes seemed to favor the Norwegians in 1938, when Sigurd Ulland of Lake Tahoe, California—the national ski champion and Pacific Northwest ski champion—broke the national jump record, soaring 236 and 249 feet.

An editorial in the *Echo* on February 3, 1938, emotionally outlined Leavenworth's achievements in holding high the torch of skiing—by building the ski hill, by persevering during the two years when there was insufficient snow by hauling snow to the hill in apple boxes and packing it down, and by leading in the organizing of recreational ski clubs.

Skiing in all its forms was rapidly gaining popularity, and manufacturers responded with more efficient equipment. The most important changes were the improvements in secure bindings. In the 1920s and 1930s, bindings were crude and unreliable, consisting first of a bent-metal toepiece and straps, then a cable device to push the boot forward more securely, and finally a Bildenstein binding, which would release if the skier had a bad fall. Just before the 1956 Olympics, a binding pioneered by racer Hannes Marker was introduced, one that would release sideways. Today, highly sophisticated, safe releases are standard.

For greater control, ski manufacturers began to add metal edges to skis. Boots evolved from hiking-boot styles to today's rigid plastic boots that are molded to one's foot. In the late 1920s, ski pants were bell bottoms. Austrian and American racer Franz Gabl of Bellingham says that Olympic contestants used to put shoelaces around their ankles to keep their pants from flopping. Gradually ski pants became slimmer, jackets lighter and warmer, until the stretch suit of today was adopted.

Increasing numbers of ardent skiers were coming to Stevens Pass to walk up slopes and ski down. Magnus Bakke and Walter Anderson became leaders of the effort to develop a Stevens Pass ski area, working with the Wenatchee and Everett chambers of commerce and with Gilbert Brown and Walter Lund of the Wenatchee National Forest. Del McCracken was the first president of Stevens Pass Recreation Association, the organization promoting the ski area. With chamber, corporate, and private donations, the group, including the Stevens Pass Company (the future commercial operators of the ski area), purchased 121 acres of land-grant property from Northern Pacific and gave it to the USFS for a ski area in 1936. At the time John Parkhill was president of the Wenatchee Ski Club.

Don Adams and Bruce Kehr, on-site operators and owners of the ski area facilities, personally worked like draft horses to get the area equipped. With dense second-growth timber on the hill, crews starting from top and bottom cut a slot through the trees. When waist-high snags were left, Kehr and Adams personally leveled them to the ground to make the terrain suitable for skiing. Then the owners installed an 800-foot rope tow powered by a Ford V-8 engine located in a temporary shed, later a two-story tow house, on the lower left side of Big Chief Mountain. Adams and his bride, Blanche, honeymooned at the crude building, despite rough winter weather. Kehr's wife, a city girl named Virginia, learned to ski and eventually became one of Washington's best powder skiers. The tow opened that winter, in 1937–38, but the west-side road was not kept open in winter, and Wenatchee skiers venturing to the summit claimed the hill was too steep. The gross sales that season were $80; insurance cost $87.

The Stevens Pass Company used generators for power and tapped into Jake Beattiger's power plant on Tye River until the Chelan Public Utility District commenced service to Stevens Pass, Inc., in 1955. This made possible the first night skiing that same year.

Construction started in the summer of 1937 on a ski hut. Designed by USFS architects Allen S. Cary and George W. Dennis, the hut measured thirty by eighty feet, including two large warming rooms, a kitchen, lavatories, waxing rooms, and caretaker's quarters. Like Leavenworth's lodge, it was made of natural wood and stone, with handsome stonework by Magnus Bakke. Because Civilian Conservation Corps labor was used, the hut was completed for less than $2,500. It was dedicated on December 4, 1938.

Skiers used the rope tow, or enjoyed long cross-country or easy downhill trails, or climbed 2,000 feet to Barrier Ridge, or trekked to Big Chief Headwall, Skyline Lake, or even Lake Josephine for a subsequent exciting descent. Under president Walker Pickens, the Wenatchee Ski Club held the first-ever slalom race at Stevens and organized the first ski carnival. Del McCracken persuaded some skiers to drive to Scenic and take the train to Berne, where he met them with an old bus and cars to haul them to the summit. About 4:00 P.M. the skiers left for Scenic on skis, using the snow-covered highway, which was not open in winter at that time.

On March 13, 1938, Stevens Pass ski area was formally dedicated by members of the Everett and Wenatchee ski clubs. The GNR ran special ski trains for the first time; it continued to do so for years thereafter, with skiers leaving the train at Berne. The Summit Inn served lunch and dinner to dignitaries, including GNR officials who were considering opening another ski area, on Mill Creek, to be served by rail.

The Mill Creek site had been the brainchild of McCracken and friends. The plan was for a Sun Valley–style destination resort, to be entered through the old Mill Creek shaft used in construction of the Eight-Mile Tunnel; no cars or buses would be allowed. Then the planners realized the site would be in a heavy avalanche area.

During the winter of 1938–39, the Scenic Highway was kept open from the east to the summit and from the west to Scenic, accommodating an average of 500 skiers per day on weekends. West-side skiers took the train from Scenic to Berne. On February 26, 1939, the Everett and Wenatchee ski clubs held the second annual ski carnival.

Unfortunately, the newly built ski hut burned on January 15, 1939, the fire possibly starting in an improperly designed fireplace. Although the flames were detected early, there was no fire-fighting system to stem them. There was no money available to fund a rebuilding effort, but the government offered the labor of the Icicle Camp Civilian Conservation Corps. Individuals, the Wenatchee and Everett chambers of commerce, and the ski clubs joined in raising $12,000 to buy the materials, and the new lodge was reopened in December 1940. Built according to a design similar to the original one and using Magnus Bakke's undamaged stone-work, the lodge is still there today.

In October 1939, volunteers from seven ski clubs, including the Everett and Seattle Mountaineers, helped the commercial operators to complete three improvements: a ski track from the head of the slalom course to Big Chief cirque, a better downhill course from Hemlock to Ski Bowl, and a run toward Grace Lakes.

In 1941, the annual ski carnival added glamour to its festivities in the form of a ski carnival queen and princesses. The first queen was Winifred Byron of Everett; the first princesses were Betty Andrews of Cashmere and Mary Wine of Wenatchee. The operators hosted races with obstacles like hay bales or water holes, as well as an estimated-time race; one year ski instructor Jack Nagle came within one-half second of his estimated time. Many skiers wore crazy costumes.

Fortunately for the ski area, the federal government considered rec-reation essential during World War II, sending Army and Navy person-nel to Stevens Pass for R&R and providing gasoline for operating the rope tows. Both Adams and Kehr went to war, but the ski area remained open with the help of a nonmilitary friend and the owners' wives. The highway to the summit was kept plowed as part of the military road sys-tem, and from the east the road was usually open anyway, if slippery. During the 1940 ski season, numerous private clubs, including the Friars (today called the Swiss Ski Club), the Everett Ski Club, the Penguins, and The Mountaineers, either acquired land or started construction of their own lodges. Only the lodges begun by the Penguins, the Everett Ski Club, and the Friars were completed before World War II. The Seattle Mountaineers completed its lodge in 1947, Bremerton Ski Cruisers in 1946, and Stevens Pass Ski in 1947. A mile-long T-bar lift was built along the route now occupied by the Barrier chair; it proved very popular with skiers, who paid fees of $2.75 per day to use it.

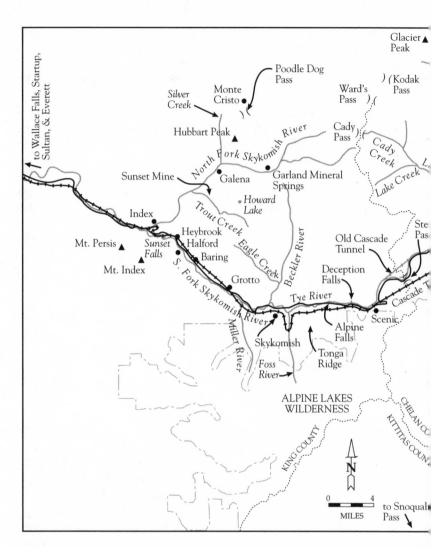

Between 1940 and 1947, the Stevens Pass Company built nine rope tows and added a ski shop with rentals, operated by concessionaires Osborn & Ulland.

In the late 1940s, it became obvious to Adams and Kehr that a chair lift would be desirable at their ski area. The chair lift had been invented by Jim Curran, an engineer for the Union Pacific Railroad, who had been designing trams for loading bananas. His first designs for Sun Valley,

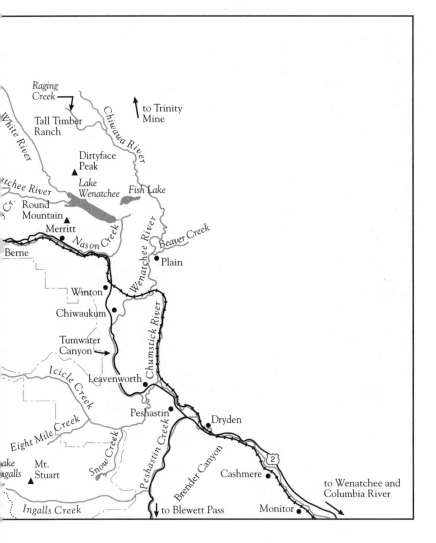

Idaho, were considered too dangerous but were later accepted by the resort's consultant, Charles Proctor; the first chair lifts were placed in service in 1936.

Adams and Kehr traveled to Sun Valley to look at the chair lifts with rubber-tired wheels made by a firm called Riblet Tramway of Spokane. The firm had built the 1,200- to 1,500-foot tram at Grotto that carried limestone down to Portland Cement Company's Grotto plant, and earlier it had built ore trams for mines. It had also built a chair that ran on steel wheels at Mount Hood shortly after World War II.

Adams and Kehr asked Riblet to engineer a double chair lift for Stevens Pass like the ones at Sun Valley. Kehr says it was a "do-it-your-self chair-lift kit" because, to save money, the two men contracted for the design, engineering, and parts but physically built the first chair themselves with hand labor. The supporting towers consisted of four poles each, with big timbers as crosspieces. This Barrier chair lift, which opened in 1953, was immediately preferred by most skiers, so Stevens Pass Company began phasing out rope tows. In 1955–56, the Blue chair lift was designed with single pylon towers like those used today. By 1960, the Seventh Heaven chair was operating, and by 1976 there were seven chair lifts and no further rope tows.

The Stevens Pass Company took on a third partner, Seattle attorney John Caley, in 1947. Caley, Bruce Kehr, and others bought out Don Adams in 1960, and the company then became Stevens Pass, Inc. (SPI).

In 1960–61, the National Downhill and Slalom Championships were held at Stevens Pass, and in 1962 and 1963, the pass hosted the National Professional Skiers race. The latter attracted such famous skiers as Pepi Gramskammer (who finished first in the event one year), Christian Pravda, Stein Eriksen, and Anderl Molterer.

The meteoric rise of skiing in the 1930s also gave impetus to those lobbying to have Stevens Pass Scenic Highway become a state highway. The funds available for maintaining and plowing the highway in winter were inadequate. It was clear that tourism and ski jumping at Leavenworth, the developing ski area at Stevens Pass, and the need for access to the wilderness by the USFS all exacerbated the pressure for appropriations to improve the scenic but narrow, largely dirt road. Back in March 1929, a bill to make the road a state primary highway failed in committee, but the promoters of the highway (including Pete Heming and Fred Morgan of the Stevens Pass Highway Association, and Lieutenant Governor John Gellatly) did manage to extract $424,600 for improvements.

Backers were delighted when the GNR rerouted its tracks through the Chumstick Valley, abandoning the Tumwater Canyon route. This left the way clear to use the old railroad grade for Stevens Pass Scenic Highway, which would result in a significant reduction in distance between Index and Leavenworth and would be a very scenic addition, too. A mere month after trains rattled through the canyon for the last time and picked up their rails, automobiles made the grand-opening trip on September 1, 1929. Perhaps 1,000 people celebrated the opening, applauding speakers, taking photos of the canyon, and picnicking at Leavenworth City Park. Frank Kammer, in an Eaglerock airplane, and Bob Martin, with a Stinson, gave rides to the brave.

Enthusiasts still hoped that the state would include Stevens Pass in its system and would eventually pave it. Promoters talked of a giant scenic loop going from Seattle to the Tri-Cities via Snoqualmie Pass, north to Spokane, and back through Wilbur, Wenatchee, and Stevens Pass to Everett and Seattle. Among the vocal supporters at later meetings of the Stevens Pass Highway Association was famed photographer Asahel Curtis, then chairman of a Seattle Chamber of Commerce committee. An *Echo* article of March 27, 1931, began a sentence, "Now that the SP hwy is part of the state program . . ." The Stevens Pass highway was not yet so designated, however. At this time, a cutoff left the highway near Monroe to enter Seattle via Duvall and Woodinville, saving many miles. In June 1934, work ensued on better alignment of the old road with Tumwater Canyon through Leavenworth, and by August the contractor, Romano Engineering Co., had finished paving that one-mile stretch. Although it was still the Great Depression, funds for the highway had become available during this period under federal and state plans to create work for the unemployed.

All through the 1930s the improvement and realignment of Stevens Pass highway went forward, thanks to the passage of generous appropriations to support the work; unquestionably, a principal reason for the progress was the use of Works Progress Administration labor. An *Echo* headline of February 21, 1936, proclaimed, "Huge Sum for Roads"—right up there in importance beside the headline "Bill West's Hen Lays Double Egg."

The evolving state highway still followed the old GNR grade through Tye to the switchbacks, and managers considered but rejected the idea of bolstering the old Cascade Tunnel and running traffic through it in winter; the completed road was to be not less than thirty-two feet wide. This plan was not carried out, however. (Today, weather permitting, one still can veer off and follow the route as a scenic road from Scenic to the summit; one can also find segments of the original highway on the east side.)

The road was officially designated primary state highway 15 in 1937, but its completion was largely ignored. Supporters of a state highway were becoming jaded. The August 23, 1939, *Wenatchee World* ran a story on the highway using bursts of capital letters, exclaiming that there were "FIVE IMPROVED HIGHWAYS" across the Cascades in the small southern half of the state, and yet "NO FINISHED HIGHWAYS" in the

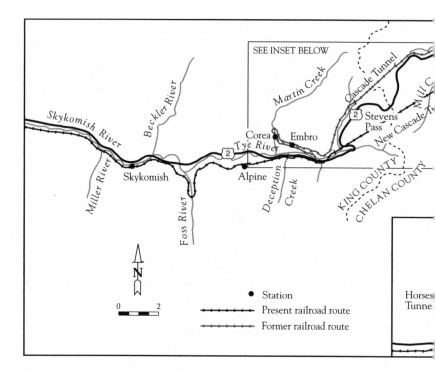

large northern half of the state: "Read it AND WEEP—you North Washington folk! Then get ready to FIGHT! You don't have to stand for any such conditions!" The article pointed out that although Chelan County and the federal government had long since completed their sections, the state kept finding reasons not to work on its segment.

In 1940, chambers of commerce on both sides of the mountain prepared a folder extolling the benefits of a decent road. Pressure from the large Stevens Pass Highway Association led, in 1940, to the designation of the pass road as an alternate of Highway 10.

Then came rumblings of World War II as well as increased use of the highway by skiers. On October 21, 1945, a big snowstorm left 300 cars stalled on Stevens Pass. There was talk of rushing Stevens Pass highway to completion as an alternate route out of Seattle that could be used if the city were bombed. A politician argued, however, that no route would cause a greater bottleneck than Stevens Pass. As late as 1947, there was an uproar over consulting engineer Ole Singstad's

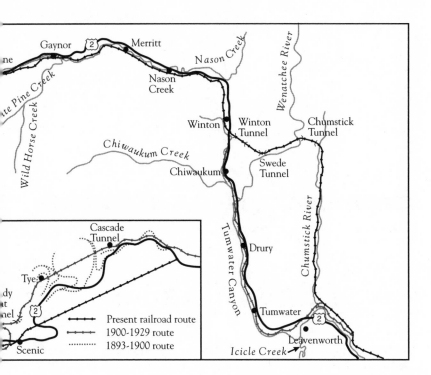

suggestion that Stevens Pass should be set aside and the state should instead build a tunnel splitting off from Ellensburg to Ritzville.

In the summer of 1949, there was intensive work on the Stevens Pass highway, and—even though World War II was over—the road *was* rushed through as an alternate escape route from Seattle. The State Highway Department declared the road completed in 1951, renaming it Stevens Pass Highway. In 1963, Stevens Pass Highway became Highway 2 and Blewett Pass became Highway 97; Highway 10 went through Snoqualmie Pass.

12. BAVARIAN TOWN

Ski jumping and later Nordic skiing continued to flourish in Leavenworth. But skiing wasn't enough to save the town from falling into an economic depression after rail and lumber interests moved on. The town became a ghostly place of empty buildings and flapping shutters, interspersed with tired shops barely hanging on.

In a demonstration of the city's spirit, the Leavenworth Improvement League, under its president, Mrs. R. B. Field, drew up a plan for eight separate civic improvement projects: the Front Street Park, turning a sand pit into a rockery, a women's clubhouse, a ski hill, a swimming pool, the Cascade Sanitarium, a golf course, and the work of the Junior Garden Club. The ambitious agenda won a 1935 *Better Homes & Gardens* Civic Beautification Tablet for Leavenworth, one of only three towns in the United States to be so recognized that year. The April 12, 1935, *Leavenworth Echo* reported the judges' comments: "Glorifying a town of 1,500 inhabitants, a town filled with much unsightliness but surrounded by great natural beauty, is no easy task, and the judges had no hesitation in awarding the coveted tablet to Leavenworth."

Another grass-roots project made life livelier. The old rail depot was moved across the street to become a grange hall in 1938. The farmers rolled the building on logs, using their own tractors. The green-roofed building was thereafter the site of lively square dancing; the building would virtually pulsate.

During the World War II years, little happened to improve the town's economy, and by the 1950s the town was in danger of total decline, although it was supported by the U.S. Forest Service, the national fish hatchery, a few loggers, the skiers, and the orchardists. In the early '50s, fire claimed Leavenworth's Anderson Hotel, and four years later the roller rink burned, recalling Leavenworth's many fires decades earlier.

So many Leavenworth residents were on welfare in the early 1960s, and prices were therefore so low, that the county actually sent other welfare recipients there to live economically. The final blow came when the state highway was widened all the way to Wenatchee. Now a leisurely trip from Wenatchee to Leavenworth took only twenty-five minutes; formerly, the hour-long drive had discouraged residents from making the trip. Leavenworth's shops were truly dying; there were twenty-four empty buildings downtown.

A handful of courageous, determined peope cast around for some solution to the town's decline—just as citizens had rallied to support their city in 1935. Among the initiators were Pauline Watson and her husband, Owen; Ted Price; and Bob Rodgers. The latter two men had purchased the Squirrel Tree Restaurant at Cole's Corner and transformed it with a Bavarian motif. They agitated for Leavenworth businesses to do something similar, but as Pauline Watson puts it, "To most people, Cole's Corner was not Leavenworth; it was *miles* away." Yet a group of enterprising residents met to organize Leavenworth Improvement for Everyone (LIFE).

The Vesta Junior Women's Club, with just twelve members, sponsored the LIFE project to study the options for Leavenworth's future and contacted University of Washington professors to serve as consultants. The Bureau of Community Development adopted Leavenworth as a study project; rather than recommend what the town should do, the agency would teach the community how to study itself.

Fully half the community worked on the ensuing study. Fifteen committees developed plans. Shirley Bowen served as the spark plug for the renewal. Ted Price insisted that there be a committee to study tourism. When all the scrutiny was completed in 1962–63, a town meeting was held, and residents decided to try an Autumn Leaf Festival, even before making any other changes. It was held in 1963. In 1964, the Vesta Club won a $10,000 national prize for the community improvement effort from the General Federation of Women's Clubs and the Sears Roebuck Foundation. The club spent the money on a new fire truck, making the presentation as part of the Autumn Leaf Festival.

As plans for renovation progressed, Price was "always talking about Solvang," says Watson, "and showed slides to five of us who were mulling

Leavenworth before and after remodeling as a Bavarian town (Photo: Special Collections Division, University of Washington Libraries, negs. 15492, 15489)

over the city's prospects." A Bavarian theme seemed possible. The idea of an alpine village had been floating around since the 1930s; the junior high school newspaper was called the *Yodeler*, and the newspaper was the *Echo*. At the time, resident Laverne Peterson was constructing what has become the Edelweiss Hotel (formerly the Chikamin) in downtown Leavenworth, and after viewing Price's slides, she declared, "Well, that's good enough for me. I will do it."

The committee gathered pictures of Europe and drew designs, assisted by Bob Rodgers and Pauline Watson, for the remodeling of five buildings. Then the promoters called a meeting of the merchants. Watson did not place undue pressure on merchants, but requested that any renovation or new construction be in a Bavarian style. There was unanimous agreement. The idea caught fire. That night the Project Alpine committee was formed, with Pauline Watson elected president, Bob Rodgers as vice president, and Evelyn Larson as secretary. The committee decided that Peterson would do her building first and glean the publicity, and the Watsons' Alpen Haus Gifts would follow. Curiously, a Solvang architect, Ed Peterson (no relation to Laverne), visited Leavenworth about this time. He drew up some designs for the Edelweiss and freely gave valuable advice to townspeople on such issues as the problems caused by snow and ice on alpine-style roofs, the necessity of doing stucco work before frost, and special timbering needs.

The old brick buildings of Leavenworth were solid but needed updating to meet fire and building codes. According to Watson, the city council feared that the addition of steep roof lines, balconies over the sidewalk, and wood decor would drastically increase fire-insurance rates. The exasperated Project Alpine committee went as a body to talk personally with the state insurance commissioner. The commissioner was willing to help, and sent personnel to Leavenworth. One by one, the problems were ironed out.

As construction began, concurrent with such special events as the Autumn Leaf Festival, Ted Price's public-relations connections in Seattle proved invaluable. Stories of the transformation appeared in local, regional, and then national magazines and newspapers. Heinz Ulbricht, who had moved to Tacoma from Freiburg, West Germany, read about Leavenworth's effort. He was a designer who had engineered some small theme projects. He contacted the Watsons, who met with him on a Friday, showed him their plans for Alpen Haus, and asked for suggestions—even though the contractors were due to start on Monday. Ulbricht was in Leavenworth Monday with proposed changes, which the Watsons adopted. He became so interested that he stayed on to help with the design of the Edelweiss Hotel and other buildings, and eventually made Leavenworth his home. He designed Leavenworth's Seafirst Bank, the Stroup Building, the Brownlee Building, Norris Hardware, the Marketplatz, and the Cafe Christa, named for his wife.

Since the Edelweiss construction was not progressing quickly, the Watsons' Alpen Haus opened first, just to get things moving. Other businesses remodeling with a Bavarian theme included Larsen's Drug Store and two buildings bought and remodeled by Ted Price and Bob Rodgers, which became Tannenbaum's and a bakery. Painter Herb Schraml did many of the paintings on building interiors.

To promote their town, Bavarian-clad residents staffed a booth at Seattle Center in 1966, exhibiting scale models of Leavenworth buildings and touting the Autumn Leaf Festival. In 1967, Leavenworth gained national fame when *Look* magazine presented it with the All-American City Award.

As the alpine theme grew, Watson and Rodgers became watchdogs of authenticity. "Some people thought just hanging out a few baskets would do it," says Watson, "but we wanted and have kept authenticity. We even talked some businesses into postponing remodeling until they could afford to do a harmonious makeover." All the town's large neon signs came down in 1969 and were replaced by small, wooden, carved signs.

The city established a design review board. There would be no neon, no backlit signs, no plastic. The size of signs would be governed by building size. Any commercial buildings seen from the highway would be of Bavarian architecture and have the design and paint motif approved. Even though the design review board was made up of volunteers, some of them went to Europe and studied authentic Bavarian architecture.

By the 1970s, the renovation of Leavenworth had succeeded beyond anyone's wildest dreams. New ideas continued. At first, merchants used plastic flowers in their baskets, believing real flowers would not thrive in the heat. Resident Karen Dean objected and talked merchants into planting tubs and hanging baskets with flowers. When she opened a gallery, she planted her lot with real flowers. Little by little, others followed her example. The hanging baskets became spectacular. Fisher Geraniums of Germany was contacted to do research on which varieties would grow well. Fisher sent over 6,000 geranium plants free of charge, and the town gave them out to businesses who would plant them. The flowers began to look better and better, and merchants discovered that a young orchard worker was coming in after work to pluck dead blooms off and add plant food—all voluntarily and without fanfare. The young man was hired to care for the town's flowers.

Leavenworth's fame continues to grow and grow: today it is an internationally known destination, expanding mildly but never losing sight of its authenticity. The Royal Bavarians, official ambassadors for Leavenworth, host major town events in costume and enter parades to promote the town—all at their own expense. Frequent festivals bring busloads and carloads of visitors, and the Christmas Lighting Festival of early December brings viewers by special Burlington Northern train—much as in the days of the ski-jumping events. The Autumn Leaf Festival attracts as many as 35,000 visitors each year; other festivals include the Great Bavarian Ice Fest in January, Maifest, Kinderfest, and the International Folk Dance Festival.

Since 1966, Art in the Park downtown has featured the works of up to fifty artists. A twenty-five-bell carillon plays intermittently every day during festivals and during the summer. The famed Marlin Handbell Ringers perform in the street from time to time, particularly during the Christmas season, when the Village Voices, a choral group, also charms visitors. At a local hotel, reveille is sounded each morning on an alpenhorn. The imaginative "bootstrap" efforts of Leavenworth's residents from 1932 to the present surely saved their town from stagnation and decline.

THE WEST SIDE

13. INDEX AND SKYKOMISH

Due to the hostile winter climate, the snow-choked western slopes of Stevens Pass never hosted any Indian groups permanently, although Skykomish Indians did hunt along the North Fork of the Skykomish, and they berried near Stevens Pass. In a letter on file at the Leavenworth Ranger Station, Norman Lenfest of Snohomish, a great-great-grandson of speculator E. C. Ferguson (who, with engineer E. F. Cady, built a trail toward Cady Pass), wrote that the Indians said they used an Indian trail over the pass to go to eastern Washington.

The Skykomish were separate from but similar to the Snohomish Indians. Studies for the Indian Claims Commission assert there was a potlatch village along the north bank of the Skykomish River, near the junction of the north and south forks (where Index lies today). Local people have found many arrowheads, now displayed in the small Index Museum. Probably due to past floods, no signs of structures remain. Ethnographers mention one upriver band, called "fern people," who lived in the Skykomish and Foss river areas above Index. There is an artifact site, a cavelike dwelling thought to be a way station en route to hunting areas, two miles west of Skykomish. There researchers found a few arrowheads and salmon parts in a form that suggested they had been packed in, perhaps in dried bundles.

Skykomish tribal member William Martin told anthropologist Colin Tweddell that the name of the Index site was *x>xausalt*, a word meaning "sawbill duck." The large potlatch house at the site was a base for hunters going above Index, and a smokehouse was built there especially for doctoring the sick. The Indians at Index, according to a study by Colin Tweddell, "were the genuine Skykomish tribe, rather wild; they would come up in canoes and suddenly [be] gone, hid in the rocks by Index . . . were fast walkers—would go way over Three Sister Peak beyond Baring and back to Index in one day picking berries."

Available estimates suggest that the Skykomish population was small. In 1853 there were said to be about 175 Skykomish; in 1881, 155; and in 1900, 320 around Sultan and Gold Bar, all intermarried among forty families. The U.S. government, which at that time considered the tribe to be part of the Snohomish people, officially appointed William Stay-shat-til, or Steh-shail, as subchief of the Skykomish on March 28, 1856.

Families moved with the food-gathering cycles, generally berrying in the area where the towns of Snohomish and Lake Stevens lie today, huckleberrying at Stevens Pass, hunting in the Pilchuck and Sultan areas, and conducting seasonal hunts above Index for mountain goat, deer, and bear. It is believed that the Skykomish made hats from goat's wool. Young men sought spirit power around Stevens Pass and Lake Getchel.

Seven members of the Skykomish Indians signed the Treaty of Point Elliott on January 22, 1855, and the tribe soon moved to the Tulalip Reservation, melting into the Snohomish tribe so thoroughly that, when Indian claims were negotiated in the 1960s, the government at first denied compensation to the Skykomish, refusing to recognize them as a distinct tribal identity. After the Snohomish filed an appeal to the Court of Claims on August 27, 1965, on behalf of the Skykomish, a settlement was made for the Snohomish and Skykomish as separate tribes.

Apparently the Skykomish Indians were not in evidence in 1874, since there is no mention of them in writings from that period. In that year, prospecting fever began north of Index, around Silver Creek. That year, near the head of the creek, Hans Hanson made the first mineral discovery, which he called the Norwegian, and carved the name of the claim and the date on a tree. His claim ran up the mountain from a point 500 feet above the forks of the creek. Soon a man named Johnson discovered an outcropping of iron pyrites. Mistaking it for gold, he rushed to Snohomish with the news, causing a stampede of loggers seeking their fortunes. About fifty claims were quickly filed on Silver Creek. Johnson persuaded E. C. Ferguson, Theron Ferguson, Lot Wilbur, and W. M. Whitfield to spend $2,000 to $3,000 to build an ore-processing facility near Mineral City. Located at the junction of the north and south forks of Silver Creek, Mineral City was merely a way station with not even a horse trail.

In those days, prospectors packed everything to the site on their backs, presumably up the Skykomish along Cady's old bushwhacked trail. Old writings also indicate that there may have been another trail from Wallace (now Startup) that went north and east, more or less following the Sultan River toward Mineral City. Around Wallace the largest claim being developed was part of the estate of Lydia E. Pinkham (of the patent medicine family). The Pinkham claim was named "The 45" because 45 men worked there. Activity accelerated in 1882, when Elisha H. Hubbart cut a trail to a camp near Mineral City that he called Galena. He filed the Anna, Trade Dollar, and Morning Star claims.

In 1889, Amos D. Gunn and his wife, Persis, bought a homestead at Index from a man named Scott. Persis named Mount Index, Mount Persis, and Gunn's Peaks, east of Index. The Gunns expanded their homestead to accommodate wayfarers, since Index in 1893 was a convenient place to leave the new Great Northern Railroad and get outfitted for the trip north to Silver Creek. The site was a natural place for a town. Only Index and Skykomish would be able to claim stability as "towns" on the west side of Stevens Pass; other settlements were railroad or logging camps (see Chapter 6).

A real boom developed all around Index. Joseph Pearsall, a Mineral City prospector with some knowledge of geology and minerals, followed an outcrop up Hubbart's Peak in 1889. At the summit he surveyed the surrounding country with binoculars and noticed an extensive ledge of galena glittering along a steep wall of a valley to the north. He was able to travel through present-day Poodle Dog Pass, actually an alpine cirque, and descend into the well-like Monte Cristo valley. He marveled at an entire mountain of galena. Sharing his exciting information with his friends Frank Peabody and John MacDonald Wilmans, Pearsall had samples of ore assayed. The results were favorable, and the three men quietly went about filing claims.

By 1890 the news could no longer be contained, and the rush was on. Prospectors swarmed in. In response to its location as a crossroads, Galena was platted in 1891 as a town site. A formidable phalanx of mountain peaks separated Monte Cristo from Galena and Index, however. Prospectors not fighting for claims in Monte Cristo were able to explore from rail-accessible Index because a good horse trail and then a wagon road was developed north to Galena. Prospectors spread out easterly, too, toward Cady Pass and on into the Beckler River area north of Skykomish.

A list of the many claims in the area would include Sunset, Evergreen, and Oro Fino. The same Monte Cristo mineral ledge extended south into the area of Troublesome Creek, a tributary of the North Fork of the Skykomish, leading to dozens more claims such as Daisy, Corona, and Great Scott.

In 1895, a great copper ledge was discovered by Frank Bleakley and Charles Shepp, who filed the Anaconda group of four claims; it too was cut and exposed by the river.

At first, mining engineers scoffed at the ores of the area as broken and of little depth. Prospectors concentrated on free gold at the mouths of creeks but passed by the ledges of sulphide ore heavily capped with oxidized iron, which they found toward the mouth of the creek, and went on toward its source, where they found galena. Later discoveries showed that the ore they ignored was not silver but gold and copper, and that the iron caps disguised rich ledges.

In his 1897 book *Mining in the Pacific Northwest*, mining engineer Lawrence Hodges described the ore bodies:

> Near the head of the creek [Silver] the ore is copper and iron sulphides carrying gold and silver, but as the mineral belt is followed down the creek silver-bearing galena appears, as in the Morning Star, and by the Vandalia and Lockwood groups. Silver and lead predominate in this form, gold and copper taking second place. Within half a mile below the Vandalia, however, the character of the mineral again changes, and to the Michigan group, the Anaconda and Oro Fino, gold and copper take first place and lead and silver are the lower values. The ledges generally contain pay streaks of high enough value to be profitably shipped to the smelter if the wagon road were extended to Silver Lake.

The Howard group of eleven claims was being developed below Howard Lake. "A sixteen foot tunnel is in ore all the way" in one of several parallel ledges, Hodges wrote. He described other claims including Copper, Iron Mountain (owned by the Iron Mountain Consolidated Gold and Copper Mining Company), Commercial, and Lost Creek.

One of the wonders of the area was a natural tunnel near the head of Eagle Creek. There were three parallel ledges cut by the creek, one of which was "prospected by nature in a peculiar manner." A tunnel 165 feet long, 15 feet high, and 20 feet wide was found to run through a porphyry dike almost straight into the mountain, and on the roof and walls were streaks of high-grade copper pyrite in large crystals carrying gold and silver.

Across the Skykomish on the south side of the valley, the claims went on along the Miller River, Money Creek, and Blue Lake. Prospecting near Berlin began with the laborers building the railroad. Six miles from the GNR was the chief producing mine, one that actually made shipments—the Coney group, owned by the Baltimore & Seattle Mining & Reduction Company, at the head of Coney Creek. Forty tons of ore were shipped in 1895, returning $58.70 per ton after expenses and freight. Twenty men were employed there. The Apex mine, discussed in Chapter 6, was also in operation. Color extended on south into the Snoqualmie drainage.

Only one mile from the GNR, two miles south of the town of Index, were two claims called the Pride of Index, developed by Lot Wilbur and others of Snohomish. Also two miles south of Index, on a small stream coming into the main Skykomish River, was the Alpha group of claims. Numerous other claims were immediately adjacent to the GNR and to Index.

To serve the mining community, the Colby-Hoyt Syndicate was building and expanding a smelter in Everett. The Everett and Monte Cristo Railway Company started construction of a railroad through the Stillaguamish River canyon to tap the genuinely rich Monte Cristo mines. The details of this exciting period are in the fine book *Monte Cristo* by Philip R. Woodhouse (The Mountaineers, 1979).

Meanwhile, another "gold mine" was identified along the Cady Trail—a medicinal hot springs, later known as Garland Hot Springs. The settlement around the springs, one of the earliest in the area, was acquired by Dr. J. N. Starr, who had come from Chicago in search of a warmer climate and better air to cure his wife of tuberculosis of the knee. Happening to hear from a transient Englishman about the springs, which were said to be better than those at Baden Baden, Germany, Starr traveled to what he named Starr Hot Springs, built a cabin, and returned to Snohomish for his wife, who was in such pain that she could scarcely travel to the springs. After two baths daily for three weeks, Mrs. Starr was delighted to have no further pain at all. Starr proceeded to secure title to the lands under a grant from President Grover Cleveland in May 1896.

U.S. Forest Service cultural resource personnel postulate that Skykomish Indians may have come to the springs, because there are extensive ocher deposits nearby, popular with the Indians for decoration and even as a sunburn preventative.

After Starr died, in the 1930s the property came into the hands of Burt Garland, who built a resort consisting of a twenty-room hotel with a twenty-tub bathhouse and doctor's treatment rooms in the basement; several modern, furnished cabins; at least one 45-by-100-foot swimming pool, and other accommodations. Garland sold the resort around 1946 to Ralph Taylor, who continued to operate it. Included in the activities were dancing and gambling. Sailors used the resort for R&R during World War II. In 1953, Taylor sold the resort to the Reverend Cameron A. Sharpe, who operated it as a Christian resort and conference center. Unfortunately, the hotel burned down in the 1950s, and the flow of the springs diminished.

As mentioned earlier, Index bloomed during the prospecting period as a GNR stop. The Gunns formally platted Index on April 25, 1893, just in time to have it burn down on July 22—the town then consisting of just a hotel, a general store, and a few residences. The fire started when a boy, reading in bed, overturned a candle. Earlier in the year, Everett Terminal Land & Milling Company and speculator Henry Hewitt, Jr., had both obtained significant real estate holdings in the settlement. Hewitt was also said to have a controlling interest in Galena.

Occupants rebuilt by the following year and prospered, since GNR's tracks passed the town site. By 1897, a second store, owned by Andrew J. Indredson, and the inevitable saloon had come to Index, but there still was no wagon road to the town; everything came by rail, and then by trail, north to the mines. Soon there were amenities such as lodging houses, more hotels, a barbershop, a drugstore, an assay house, the Sunset Falls Lumber plant, and restaurants. In 1902, another fire burned half

The only truly active mine near Index was the Sunset Mine. (Photo: Special Collections Division, University of Washington Libraries, neg. Pickett 4444)

of the business area, starting in the Sunset lodging house, but the resilient owners rebuilt. The population at this time was around 1,000, and Index was called "the Butte of Washington." The *Index Miner* of April 5, 1900, declared that a contract had been let to Sheppard & Henry for building a branch railroad to go from Hamilton (in the Skagit Valley) up the Sauk River to Monte Cristo and then through a tunnel to Index. The railroad was never built, however.

In 1903, a squabble between the owners of Sunset Falls Lumber Company turned ugly; pending settlement of the dispute, a guard, Barney Corbett, was stationed in the mill. While he was briefly absent from the mill, an unknown person, suspected to be one of the disgruntled partners, placed dynamite in the mill stove. When Corbett built a fire later, the resultant explosion was heard for miles and wrecked the office. Corbett was uninjured but furious.

Despite this fracas and a couple of murders—crimes of passion— Index was a fairly peaceful frontier town, encouraging sensible entrepreneurs. Businesses in 1906 included Baitinger & Ulrich, general merchandise, who also ran pack services to the mines; C. E. Lewis, meats and groceries; C. R. Redding, drugs and assay office; the Bush House; the Index Hotel, owned by Bennett & Howard in 1900; the Grand Pacific Hotel; the Perigalli; Ross Phillips, confectioner; and the *Index Miner* newspaper, established in 1899 with C. W. Gorham as editor. In 1907, the town of Index was incorporated.

The richest mine in the Index area was the Sunset mine, about ten miles above Index. It was capitalized at $2 million in 1903 and had already shipped 300 tons of 9-percent ore from its thirteen claims of twenty acres each. Sunset's owners built a three-section wooden tram from the mine to the GNR, enabling ore to make a swift exit to Everett's new smelter. Yet the 1910–11 *Copper Handbook* reported tersely that the mine was "Dead." The property had been sold to Frank L. Bell and W. W. Black, formerly of Index, for $40,000. It lay idle for years, then was sold to E. A. Sims, who installed considerable equipment and operated it profitably.

How long the Sims management continued is unknown, but in 1917, George Stevenson and associates reopened the mine, inspired by the high World War I prices for copper, and made several improvements. In 1919, the base area had a 100-ton concentrator crusher, a ball mill, table classifiers and a flotation unit, a crew house, food service, a thirty-inch wood stove, a water pipeline, and a power compressor. (The mine was not in production in time to take advantage of the good prices, however.) The company added an access road to its workings in 1920, abandoning the tram.

The mine's output increased from 670,000 pounds in 1923 to 1,200,000 pounds in 1929, making the mine the largest copper producer in the state. The ore was shipped to the Tacoma Smelter. The November 1928 issue of *Washingtonian* magazine reported that Edward C. Morse was the superintendent of the Sunset Copper Company and that the mine was about to start up again, so there must have been at least one interruption in operation during this period.

Probably because of the downturn of demand during the Depression, the mine became unprofitable and was leased in 1936 to the Sunset Syndicate Corporation. In 1938 it was said to be operating under lien for unpaid wages to its workers, and its creditors foreclosed on August 18, 1938. After two additional turnovers, each at a lower sales price, the gale winds of 1948 caused such damage to the workings that there was no hope of reopening. Still, Sunset had proved to be the most consistently producing mine of the area.

A new enterprise came to Index in 1904—the Western Granite Works owned by John Soderberg, from which came the granite for the steps of the state capitol building in Olympia, trim and foundation for Everett's Federal Building, and curbing for Seattle's streets. T. S. Ellis opened another granite quarry a half mile east of Index in 1902. Since the quarry was adjacent to the railroad, its output was easily loaded for transport to Seattle.

In the first decade of the 1900s, more enterprises came to Index. The Sylvester Smith lumber company opened. Fraternal lodges were organized: the Independent Order of Redmen, Odd Fellows Lodge, and Rebekah Lodge. Both the Redmen and the Odd Fellows met in the Redmen's Wigwam building, built in 1902 (named a historic site in the 1970s). The *Index Miner* thrived briefly, replaced by the *Index News* in 1907; the *News* was combined with the *Skykomish Valley Star* after 1919.

The most famous and enduring of the area's hotels was the Bush House, still operating today. Its long and colorful history began in 1898. In those days the GNR conductor announced "Bush House" as a scheduled stop, and passengers were met by Mrs. Clarence Bush herself. The hotel register of November 17, 1908, lists Theodore Roosevelt, T. H. Taft, W. J. Bryan, and C. R. Redding, although some wonder if the listings were spoofs. A news clipping verifies that Bryan, at least, was there.

A guest smoking in bed started a fire in 1934 and had to be pulled out of the room by a passerby, but the fire was extinguished. Yet the hotel ceased operations about this time, occupied only by various owners—Doolittle, LeClaire, Bingham, Manzie—until 1975, when retirees Bynum and Maureen Sutton bought the Bush House and restored it over

Mount Index and Mount Persis, with the tiny railroad shelter at Heybrook in the foreground (Photo: Special Collections Division, University of Washington Libraries, neg. Pickett 3013)

a few years, retaining antiques squirreled away in the old building and an alleged poltergeist that opened a particular door each night. Today the hotel and restaurant still operate and together are considered to be the oldest business in Snohomish County.

Index's most illustrious resident may have been historical photographer Lee Pickett, who came as a shop photographer and, ten years later, became the GNR's official photographer, assigned to document the building of the railroad's Eight-Mile Tunnel. The subjects of his photographs range from the minute details of machinery and industries in the area to magnificent scenery and historical subjects. Sometimes he tinted the black-and-white prints to enhance the scenes. Pickett was an avid, capable mountain climber and guided the Seattle Mountaineers on one climb of Mount Index. The area is still a favorite rock-climbing area for The Mountaineers.

After the GNR job was finished, Pickett did general photographic projects and also worked at the Anacortes shipyards during both world wars. Following World War II he did not return to his art, claiming that the darkroom chemicals had injured his health. He and his wife Dorothy, a teacher for thirty years, continued to make Index their home. After Pickett's death, Dorothy donated his huge photographic collection to the University of Washington; the collection is still not fully cataloged.

Index resident Ruth Burgstahler, in a short history of the town, wrote that the old-timers used to gather at what was called the "anxious bench" in front of the general store to talk and reminisce. One local character was Molly Lilly, a very large woman with an appetite for liquor that matched her size. Sober she was the town's good samaritan, a kindly person. Drunk it took several deputies to subdue her and take her to jail to sleep it off. Once, when under the influence, she tore the door off her own refrigerator and threw it out in the street. Ole the Hobo shared the limelight with Lilly; he was shunted from town to town as he "slept it off" in their jails. He finally hanged himself in Index.

Despite good railroad transportation, the residents of Index were isolated in their beautiful valley. The arrival of the daily local train, nicknamed the Dinky, was the major excitement of the day. Residents met to talk, to see who came and went, to get mail and goods they had ordered from the outside world. There were a few tourists coming too, for the excellent fishing and hiking. Burgstahler recalled that when a movie theater came in 1910, it added a new dimension to her life. She especially enjoyed Pearl White's serial movies.

After a road (of sorts) to Index was completed in 1915, residents purchased cars, giving them the freedom to travel to Everett and Seattle. Later, the townspeople were deeply involved in lobbying for Stevens Pass Scenic Highway.

Since the mines, except for the Sunset Copper Company, were largely dead by the second decade of the century, it was logging and milling plus tourism that kept Index afloat until 1917, when two floods ravaged the town. The swollen Skykomish River undermined riverside residences and business houses, collapsing them into the river, and surged into town to invade homes. For a time the town was isolated because the Skykomish River bridge was destroyed.

World War I and the departure of able-bodied men paralyzed Index's few industries, but in the 1920s the Sunset Copper mine still employed about 75 men, and Sylvester Smith's mill, called the Index-Galena Logging Company after 1907, supported perhaps 150. In 1922, Index-Galena operated about fourteen miles of logging railroad along the south side of the Skykomish River, using two locomotives and flatcars. The Index mill running "one side" (the equipment necessary to process a log into lumber) had a circular head-rig, a dry kiln, a lath mill, and three shingle machines. There was a machine shop, a commissary, and an electric plant. With their families, this work force added up to about 800 residents for Index. Several other mining companies maintained headquarters in the town in 1926 or later, including Bunker Hill Mining & Smelter Company, Good Hope Mining Company, Homestead Copper Mining Company, Index Bornite Mining Company, Smugglers Gold Mining Company, and Trout Creek Mining Company.

The Great Depression brought change, robbing the community of its three major industries—mine, quarry, and mill. (The Dinky had already ceased operations in 1924, becoming a colorful part of the area's history.) The Northwest Portland Cement Company plant at Grotto and several nearby sawmills furnished employment for several families, however. Tourism continued as well.

In 1939, some of the town's scenic views went up in smoke with a gigantic forest fire that burned around the town for several weeks. The town itself was saved by a torrential rain. After the stagnation of business during World War II, most families were forced to leave and seek employment elsewhere. Today the town is experiencing a modest resurgence of business anchored by tourism and river rafting, with the Bush House and Restaurant, Index General Store, and Index Tavern constituting the principal businesses.

The other significant town of the area, Skykomish, began with the GNR. John Maloney, the founder and "father" of Skykomish, first worked as a packer with C. F. B. Haskell and John Stevens on the GNR's surveys. Maloney liked the Skykomish Valley and staked claims along the track route in 1890, settling at what he called Maloney's Siding with his wife, Louisa, after his survey work was completed. The first of his many enterprises was a general store to serve construction and railroad personnel, for in 1893, Skykomish became an important switching yard and west-side headquarters for operations. It was at Skykomish that helper steam locomotives were added (or taken off) for the arduous switchback section (the electric helpers through the Cascade Tunnel were changed at the town of Wellington/Tye). At the perimeter of the heavy snows of the western slopes, Skykomish was the point at which eastbound trains often decided whether or not to proceed during bad weather. By 1894, there was a Skykomish depot located in a boxcar on a siding, a machine shop, a roundhouse, coal chutes, and a water tank.

John and Louisa Maloney platted the town site of Skykomish on August 7, 1899, adding more lands to the plats between 1904 and 1930.

Maloney became the town's first postmaster and, together with George Farr, A. L. Smith, and Peter Larson (a Northwest entrepreneur with varying interests), formed the Skykomish Lumber Company in 1899 or 1900 to produce ties, lumber, and snowshed timbers for the GNR from the tall cedar groves of the valley. The company employed about a hundred men and had its own electric plant, waterworks, and eating house. The mill had a capacity of 60,000 board feet. Maloney chiefly operated a shingle mill with a capacity of 80,000 shingles daily, using twenty men. He also operated a quarry at Baring. McDavitt & Davis ran the town's first store, according to *The Coast* magazine of December 1903, contradicting sources that credit Maloney.

Another railroad man, Patrick McEvoy, came in 1897 to tend to the area's recreational needs. He has a place in history as the engineer of the first GNR passenger train over the switchbacks, in June 1893. Unfortunately, he lost an arm in a railroad accident, but he went on to found the Olympia saloon and pool hall, an establishment much patronized by his railroad buddies. He later turned the tavern over to his son Charles and a man named Oliver Dean. During Prohibition, the two changed the bar's name to the Maple Leaf Confectioners, but after the overthrow of the Volstead Act, it became the Whistling Post Tavern owned by Bryan Thompson. It is still a historic site today. The curious name derived from railroad patrons who said of Skykomish, "Some day this will just be a whistle-stop."

In 1900, with Skykomish's population growing, Frank Wandschneider (whom locals call Juan Snyder) built the Skykomish Hotel, a log structure that burned in 1902 and was promptly rebuilt as a four-story hotel and sold to D. J. Manning for $10,000; it still operates today. In 1905, John Maloney owned a fine general store, perhaps a modernized version of his 1893 store.

Meanwhile, Skykomish Lumber had built a new planing mill, a double-block shingle mill of 125,000 daily capacity, and two warehouses, protecting it all with a fire-fighting system. The company came into the hands of Bloedel Donovan Lumber Mills (BDLM) through a 1917 bequest in the will of Peter Larson. The acquisition, managed by a subsidiary company, Columbia Valley Lumber Company, included an estimated 133 million board feet of standing timber in the Skykomish Valley. J. N. Donovan, the son of BDLM's founder, was put in charge of the Skykomish mill. During World War I, Northwest lumber mills were hard pressed to meet the government's demands for ship lumber, boxes, building lumber, and cedar shingles. Any able-bodied men not drafted into the military services flocked to work in the mills. Skykomish boomed, its economy stimulated by the combination of lumber and rails, for special trains were ordered to carry shipbuilding and other lumber to eastern yards. Pioneer Patrick McEvoy's son John went to work for BDLM, progressing to the Seattle sales office as a good marketing man, where he excelled until the liquidation of BDLM on November 15, 1945.

Dr. Charles J. Simon set up a general practice and obtained a medical contract from BDLM. Other Skykomish businesses thriving in the early 1920s included Paul Fournier's Barber Shop, McEvoy's tavern, the Skykomish Hotel, Maloney's Home Store, Palm Drug of Glick Henry, Dan Hawley's Dairy, Hatley's Dairy, the Liberty Theater, Jake Beattiger's auto camp, Mitchell and Green's Apiary, and a business with the unlikely sounding name of "A. Hove, Automobile, Plumbing & Shoes Fixed." The apiary was somewhat unusual, too; it seems that rampant growths of fireweed took over after trees were cut and slash-burned, leading beekeepers to place hives on the cut lands.

A man named Hatley built the Cascadia Hotel, with handsome wood interiors and luxurious appointments. It became the center of town

The Bloedel Donovan mill at Skykomish thrived for several decades. (Photo: Special Collections Division, University of Washington Libraries, neg. Pickett 10128)

life, a place where men in well-cut suits met and mingled with lumber and rail magnates—as well as more gaudy, perfumed ladies.

Despite such islands of sophistication, Skykomish was mostly a rough-and-ready place where cows slept in the streets. There were board-walks, though; Skykomish resident James Wilson Timpe remembers that he and his friends would crawl under them to collect loose change that had fallen from the pockets of careless revelers. "We could make about twenty-five or thirty cents a day," he says. "And we would sell discarded flasks found in the bushes back to our local bootlegger for ten cents apiece."

In 1919, Skykomish became an official district headquarters for the GNR and, during and after the building of the Eight-Mile Tunnel, the town swelled with construction workers. For a time Skykomish was a truly vital link for the GNR, the place where steam locomotives were exchanged for electric engines for the trip to Wenatchee, or vice versa. An interesting contest during the town's Fourth of July celebrations was a tug-of-war between a steam engine and an electric one. The electrics always won, according to locals.

Several logging companies helped to feed the mills at Skykomish, Alpine, and elsewhere between 1900 and 1940. East of the Foss River, the Woods Logging Company had a large mill with a short track of its own at Tonga Siding on Tonga Ridge; after the mill was destroyed by fire in 1922, the mill owners moved into the Miller River drainage. Parker & Brown logged briefly north of the Tye River. In 1937, the Jearns Mill Co. operated near Skykomish, at Money Creek. There was also a Miller Logging Company, from which the USFS acquired lands in 1937. The Knutson-Nelson Logging Company logged in the Miller River drainage. While most logs came to the mill by truck, some loggers boomed logs to float down the Skykomish River—the first river system (it includes the Tye River and part of Beckler River) to be protected decades later under the state's 1977 Scenic Rivers Act.

The steep terrain of the west side of Stevens Pass and the adjacent Cascades caused a writer for BDLM's newsletter, *The Head Saw*, to exclaim:

> The exploits of Paul Bunyan were child's play when they are compared with some of the feats accomplished by the loggers who cut and deliver timber to the mill. Their territory has always been hilly and rough and now that all the so-called "easy" timber has been logged, Superintendent Forbes says he is looking around for a flock of trained eagles who can carry his lines up the grades for him.

Mill management in the early days required brawn as well as brains. Asa Smith, the mill foreman, reportedly gave one of his men a black

In its infancy Skykomish was a bustling town that served the railroad and the lumbering industry. (Photo: Special Collections Division, University of Washington Libraries, neg. Pickett 1723)

eye. Management was shocked until they learned that a new mill employee had come into the office to argue with Smith, then banged him over the head with a 2x4.

There was a good deal of joking between the several offices of BDLM. A purchasing agent complained that horse blankets sent from Bellingham were too light and way too small for their big logging horses, whereupon Bellingham employee C. W. Mason replied that he was shipping a pair that would be satisfactory, but "Having in mind the tender care given domestic animals in your neighborhood, we first thought of suggesting that this particular pair of blankets be cut bias on the gore, hem-stitched, have at least three rows of ruffles trimmed on the edges with old point lace."

Because many loggers and mill workers were Scandinavian, *The Head Saw* occasionally ran what it called "letters from Big Ole to his wife." A sample excerpt: "Yu ramamber ay vos vorken don by alyer kamp for Yack Donovan, vell von day he comen over to me and say, Ole ay tank yu batter pak op das vife and yur yunk and take das bote for plase called. . . ."

In June 1946, BDLM sold its Skykomish operation to Empire Millwork Corporation of New York; the mill's last owner was Robinson Plywood Company of Everett.

It was 1956 when the more powerful diesel engines came onto the GNR lines and displaced the electrics; this was the beginning of the shrinking of Skykomish into a virtual ghost town of about 200 residents. Tourism, the USFS, and minor logging supported them.

One of the town's memorable moments came when, after the death of a well-liked man known only as "Sunshine," it was discovered he had been a member of the infamous Dalton Gang. Another was when a train bearing both Harry Truman and Franklin D. Roosevelt stopped at Skykomish. A few residents met the dignitaries, but mostly U.S. Senator Monrad Wallgren ran interference for them.

The peaceful little town was almost lost in December 1970, when an explosion at Lu's Market threatened the business district. Only the intensive efforts of volunteer fire fighters saved the town, including the venerable Skykomish Hotel. Except for Tunnel Days, when tourists swarm through the historic town, Skykomish sleeps on, sustained by USFS employees and a handful of businesses that are patronized by skiers and vacationers—especially around August, when the wild blackberries are ripe for picking.

NATURAL RESOURCES

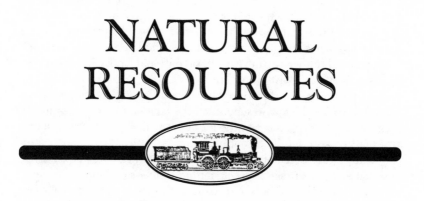

14. FORESTS AND FISH

Even before 1900, national and state governments realized the need for preservation and management of some of the vast western lands. In 1891, Congress passed the Forest Reserve Act, and in February 1897, President Grover Cleveland established districts of manageable size, including the Washington Forest Reserve (North Cascades) and the Mount Rainier Forest Reserve. Lands adjacent to Stevens Pass became the Wenatchee National Forest and, eventually, the Mount Baker–Snoqualmie National Forest. Jurisdiction was first given to the Department of the Interior and later to the Department of Agriculture under its chief forester, Gifford Pinchot. Regulation by a distant federal government was not accepted without bitter opposition, however. The *Chelan Leader* likened the move to William the Conqueror's laying waste to English lands.

Beginning in 1905, the U.S. Forest Service hired a few men as "forest guards," and in 1909, the agency devised a civil service examination for the post of forest ranger. Appointed the first supervisor of the Wenatchee National Forest in 1908 was A. H. Sylvester, who had first appeared in the area in 1897. That year he and a partner had roamed the Cascades from Snoqualmie Pass north, mapping the peaks for the U.S. Coast and Geodetic Survey team. Sylvester, a legendary USFS figure who would be remembered as the dean of the forest rangers, established a headquarters at Leavenworth and set out to patrol the forest with twenty underpaid, underequipped men.

At first a huge amount of USFS time was consumed in checking homestead claims. Then the tasks expanded into emphasis on fire detection and fire fighting. It was imperative to build foot or horse trails in order to reach blazes and examine the forests. Then as now, the USFS also managed timber-cutting permits on national lands. A forest ranger or his timber sale assistant, or "timber cruiser," traveled through the forest, estimating the amount of board feet to be sold and marking the trees to be offered. He also supervised the logging to prevent unnecessary damage to the forest. As the logs were scaled, a forest representative marked each log "U.S." with an axe.

Timber sales were important to local communities because Congress designated a percentage of receipts from timber sales and grazing permits to be used for schools and roads in the areas where the activity occurred. Vigorous marketing of timber occurred until 1958, when a timber resource review indicated that the country needed to grow more timber if it were to meet future demands for wood. Two years later, President Dwight D. Eisenhower signed the Multiple Use–Sustained Yield Act to govern USFS activities. Tree cutting has been further reduced since then; today the greater emphasis is on scientific management of the entire ecosystem. Since the 1930s, the youths of the Civilian Conservation Corps (CCC), the Job Corps, and the Youth Conservation Corps have been employed for diverse forest projects, including efforts that diminished the likelihood of destruction caused by fires.

Along the arid eastern slopes of the Cascades, forest fires could be devastating. The Wenatchee National Forest received more men during fire season. The years 1910, 1917, 1926, and 1929 were some of the worst. A frightening forest fire threatened to destroy vast timberlands in August 1924, when a logging truck exploded along the Chiwawa River (gas had dripped on its hot exhaust pipe). A fierce forest fire along a one-and-a-half-mile front ensued, with Great Northern Lumber Company workers fighting beside volunteers and forest personnel. Fortunately, there was no wind and the fire was contained to about a thousand acres by ditching around the blaze. The draft created by the fire was so great that ashes and burned-out cinders fell on the east side of the Entiat range (the Chiwawa is on the west). In 1929, by August, 49,500 acres of the Wenatchee had burned, and two fire fighters died in a fire that month.

Fire-fighting methods were pretty primitive. Lookouts did not become common until the 1920s, although the men did build a few crude platforms on high points to survey their surroundings. If the USFS detected smoke, then miners, loggers, ranchers, homesteaders, and travelers—paid personnel and volunteers alike—pitched in to beat out the flames with shovels, jackets, wet sacks, or whatever was available. In one instance, a band of sheep in a fire area was enlisted to march around and around a slow-moving fire to create a firebreak in the lush grass.

In 1911, crude telephones were installed through portions of the forest—usually just lines draped from one tree to another. They were more versatile than one might think, because with so much slack, the lines seldom broke. To make a call, the ranger simply placed a special clamp on the line almost anywhere to connect his telephone unit to the system.

The USFS then and now also managed grazing permits for the forestlands, watching for overgrazing in key grassy areas. In 1919, the *Leavenworth Echo* estimated that there were a quarter-million sheep in the Wenatchee and Chelan forests. Sheep and cattle were herded into the high country in spring and taken out before the snow fell. There were good and bad aspects to the practice; the animals kept unwanted brush down, letting sunlight shine on growing trees, but they sometimes carried vermin that spread to wild animals. In some areas, sheepmen were required to drive their flocks through sheep-dip pools before entering public forests.

The USFS was only mildly interested in recreation as a forest use initially. During the 1920s Congress did appropriate an annual sum of $7,500 to the Wenatchee National Forest for campsite sanitation and fire prevention, mostly the latter. A sharp increase in the number of tourists visiting the forests, however, made it imperative to establish at least a few campgrounds and pit toilets. According to Dennis McMillin of the Wenatchee National Forest historical overview staff at Leavenworth, early visitors often traveled to the forest in wagons, bringing along a crate or two of chickens and maybe the family cow, planning to stay for several days.

The job of a forest ranger was evolving, but just as the skills were being defined and honed, World War I came along to recruit men experienced in the same skills for the forest engineers regiment; some were assigned to harvest Olympic Peninsula spruce used for aircraft wings. The Wenatchee National Forest lost two good men to the regiment.

Drawing from his past surveying activities, A. H. Sylvester continued to attach names to key landmarks. Names were essential in order to give rangers work assignments and directions to fires. The names for which he is at least partly credited include Napeequa, the original Indian name of the North Fork of the White River (a name Sylvester restored rather than created); the Klonaqua Lakes in the Icicle watershed (*klone* means three in Chinook, and *qua* is an Indian word ending meaning water); Klone Peak, named for Sylvester's dog Klone; Doctor Creek, opposite Hoxsey Creek, both named for the pioneer physician of Leavenworth; Smithbrook, on the highway, named for H. B. Smith, the Merritt pioneer; and Cuitin Creek (*cuitin* is Chinook for horse), named for the good horse feed nearby. Sylvester adopted many other local names derived from homesteaders' locations and sheepherders' territories, adding them to his maps.

One of the most interesting names is Dirtyface Peak. An early settler, J. S. Barnard, assiduously cleared his claim at the foot of the peak. His face was often covered with perspiration-streaked soot, so fellow settlers began to call him "Dirtyface" Barnard.

In 1921, the USFS moved its headquarters from Leavenworth to Wenatchee; Sylvester remained as supervisor, though, until his retirement in 1931. About this time, the lookout stations began to gain importance in fire fighting. The first lookouts were just tree houses or platforms, with the lookout living in a nearby tent. Foresters dubbed them "rag houses." If a fire was within a reasonable distance of the lookout, he or she was expected to walk to the site and extinguish the blaze—assuming that it was not a mid-August firestorm but just a smoldering lightning strike. In 1923, a honeymooning couple was employed at the Icicle Ridge rag house. During their first night on duty, lightning struck the tent and burned all the contents, not harming the couple but subjecting them to considerable distress. By 1927, about 430 miles of telephone wire linked the lookout stations, making early warning of fire feasible. Within the Stevens Pass area were the following lookout stations:

Entiat Ranger District: Klone Peak and Sugarloaf Peak.

Lake Wenatchee Ranger District: Carne Mountain, Estes Butte, Basalt Peak, Mount David, Poe Mountain, Kodak Peak, Rock Mountain, Alpine, Dirtyface Peak, Cougar Mountain, and Soda Springs.

Leavenworth Ranger District: Chumstick Mountain, Tumwater, Lorraine Point, French Ridge, McCue Ridge, Grindstone Mountain, Icicle Ridge, and Boundary Butte.

Mount Baker–Snoqualmie Forest, Skykomish Ranger District: Benchmark Mountain, Evergreen Mountain, Proffits Point, Beckler Peak, Surprise Mountain, Mount Persis, Mount Cleveland, Maloney Mountain, Galena, Windy Point, Mount Sawyer, Sparkplug, Heybrook, and Tonga Ridge (virtually all near Skykomish).

At Stevens Pass itself: Skylight Ridge.

In the book *Lookouts*, which gives a complete and interesting account of known lookout stations, authors Ira Spring and Byron Fish tell of interesting lookout personnel. During World War I, when there was a shortage of men to work as lookouts, women were given their chance, and many women continued to do the job until lookout stations were phased out. Among the first was Iva West, who operated the Tumwater lookout from 1920 to 1922 while living in a tent. A local youth, Jimmy Burgess, was only fourteen when he undertook the responsibility at Dirtyface in 1947. He lied about his age when applying for the job, but he did commendable work for at least three years and was forgiven. Oscar Richardson manned Badger Mountain from 1953 to 1974, starting at age fifty-four.

Improvements in equipment made fire detection ever more efficient. Heliographs were purchased in 1914 and installed on at least four high lookout stations in the Wenatchee National Forest. A heliograph consisted of two mirrors placed on a tripod so they reflected each other, and a flasher that worked with a shutter to transmit Morse code a distance of up to seventy miles. When two or more lookout stations had transmitted their compass readings of a fire's location to a central Leavenworth-area station, the latter could pinpoint the location very closely, and fire fighters could save time getting there. Using flashlights at night, a heliograph's range was five to ten miles.

With the exception of the Pyramid Mountain trail from Baldy and Stormy mountains, built before 1916, most trails were hacked out by the rangers between 1916 and 1925. At first, most of the trails were intended as access roads for fire fighting and patrolling, but the USFS gradually became responsive to the growing demand for recreational trails. In just one year, 1924, the USFS accomplished a great deal: The Rainy Creek trail was opened from Stevens Pass Highway to the Little Wenatchee River near the soda springs. A trail from Dardanelles to Lake Chiwaukum was completed. The Hatchery Creek trail to the top of the mountain west of Chiwaukum was extended two and a quarter miles. Four more miles of work was done on the Icicle trail from the ranger station to Doughgod Creek. The Mad River trail was completed northward from the mouth of the Mad River to make it possible to go from the Chiwawa River to Mad Lake via Deep Creek. Finally, six miles of trail work on Jack Creek was done, as was six miles on Rock Creek and twelve miles along the White River.

Trail crews, working in steep terrain, sometimes suffered accidents. In June 1926, a man named Joe Griffiths was working with W. O. Burgess above Cougar Creek when Griffiths lost his balance and rolled down the slope. Four hundred feet below, he fetched up face-down, unconscious, in a creek. Burgess came down almost as fast to pull him out of the water and revive him. Unable to drag the injured man up the slope,

Burgess lashed him, in and out of consciousness, to a nearby tree, so he would not roll back into the creek. Then he made haste to seek help—five miles to the nearest phone. A Dr. Lessing came from Leavenworth, and rangers from the Dirtyface Ranger Station galloped to the scene on horseback. The doctor found Griffiths alive, although his skull had been crushed above his eyes and he had other bruises. Amazingly, he recovered.

In a 1932 *Pacific Crest Trailway* article, Clinton C. Clarke, an ardent conservationist from Pasadena, California, suggested that a trail be built along the mountain crests from Mexico to Canada. It would incorporate the existing 442-mile Oregon Skyline Trail and a 185-mile segment of the John Muir Trail in California. The government embraced the idea enthusiastically as a good project for the Depression-era Civilian Conservation Corps, which took young, unemployed city men and welded them into effective construction crews for the nation's forests. The entire proposed trail was surveyed. W. O. Burgess of Plain was the chief of the survey party for miles 198 to 329 in August and September 1935. Washington state's segment, the Cascade Crest Trail, was completed by 1941. Around Stevens Pass, the trail is routed along the abandoned Great Northern Railway switchbacks.

In the 1960s a commission of the Bureau of Outdoor Recreation proposed a National Trail Systems Act, which was passed by Congress and signed into law by President Lyndon B. Johnson on October 2, 1968. The law authorized the appropriation of not more than $500,000 to acquire lands for the Pacific Crest National Scenic Trail, which stitched together the various segments of high trails. The Pacific Crest Trail was essentially complete by 1980—crossing seven national parks, six state parks, twenty-five national forests, and fourteen wilderness areas. The trail's basic width of twenty-four inches widens to as much as thirty-six inches along precipitous stretches. At fifteen miles per day, it would take five months to hike the 2,400-mile trail, which stretches along some of the most spectacular crests of our nation. Bob Norton of Skykomish, now retired from the USFS, was responsible for the segments near the Stevens Pass area for many years, personally inspecting the trail frequently. He says his favorite section is from Deception Pass to Deception Lakes.

Today's hikers on the Pacific Crest Trail find huckleberries, hoary marmots, red-tailed hawks, deer, bear, and an occasional eagle near the pass. The trail is open to horseback riders, too, although Clarke himself believed only in backpacking. He was said to have ridiculed the trail-riding packhorse vacation trips organized by the Sierra Club in midcentury. Author Robert Cantwell, in a Pacific Crest Trail System publication, gave these instructions to hikers: "Start hiking early, by

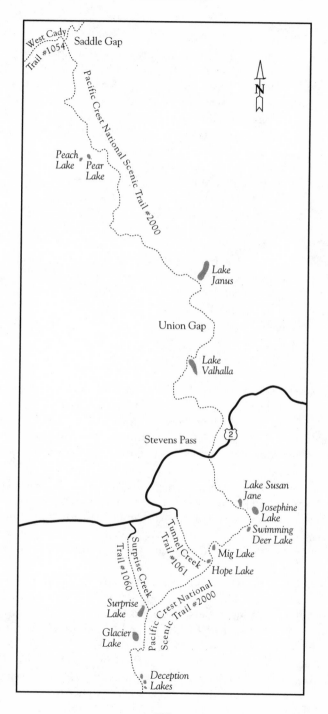

8 o'clock. Go slowly at first. Always rest by standing in the sun. (If you sit down you will lose pep.) Drink a little water, a raisin under the tongue will help." Another key figure in the Pacific Crest Trail's history, Robert Marshall—the first director of recreation for the national forests—felt that wilderness areas were to be protected not only from commercial exploitation but also from any use except hiking or horseback riding. If a person endured hardships to gain solitude, Marshall felt, so much the better.

Packer Norman Trapp, with headquarters near Merritt on the Stevens Pass Highway, was one of several professionals supplying the trail-maintenance crews in later years. An ex–rodeo cowboy of some note, Trapp came to Stevens Pass to start packing in 1960, with just six horses. He and his wife, son, and mother-in-law lived on $14 a week while he supplied food, tools, and supplies to workers on the Pacific Crest Trail and Buck Creek Pass Trail; on one trip, he provided sixty-two dozen eggs. For the Buck Creek Pass Trail, his pack train carried creosoted planks for bridges, a generator, wheelbarrows, and dynamite. In one case, he became sort of a father figure to about thirty students called "Marmots," who were on a privately sponsored program to build about four miles of new trail. He worked for The Mountaineers, the Sierra Club, and Mazamas, the latter when nine people from Harvard climbed peaks in Buck Creek Pass.

Packers come to know every nuance of the mountains and deal with every level of rider. Trapp is still at it today, assisted in recent years by his daughter Chelan. Much of his recent work has involved recreation: fishing outings, scenic camera trips to photograph wild goats, outdoor trips for celebrities like musician Tim Hardin and former *Seattle Times* photographer Josef Scaylea. When mechanized vehicles cannot reach lost hikers or airplane crash victims, packers rescue them. Several times Trapp has rescued a private party's horse that has fallen over a cliff. His worst customer, he says, "was a lady who simply had no equilibrium. She fell off twenty-eight times in a nine-mile ride, from a tame, quiet horse." Another time his party, in the mountains on September 7, endured a twenty-one-inch snowfall.

One of Trapp's predecessors as a packer was "Dude" N. L. Brown, a legendary horseman. The son of "Deak" Brown of Monitor, one of the first Wenatchee Valley settlers, Dude was handy with a gun and could ride any ornery bronc. In 1913, he gained local renown by riding an "unridable" bronc, "Kicking Dick," on a bet. During the mining era at Red Mountain, he packed supplies for the Royal Development Company, and, no doubt, took pack jobs for the USFS. He bought cattle in Tonasket and Okanogan, driving them to Wenatchee to sell at a profit;

TOP OF MT. LENNIX.
MOUNTAINEERS 5-30-15

The Great Northern Railroad and the Stevens Pass Highway made it easier for members of The Mountaineers to reach trails that led toward the high mountains. (Photo: Special Collections Division, University of Washington Libraries, neg. Pickett 6-A)

when notorious badman and cattle rustler Johnny McLean tried to take Brown's herd, Brown shot it out with McLean. No wonder, then, that he was elected sheriff of Leavenworth during the town's toughest days. What was more surprising was that locals elected this man of the saddle as their county commissioner in November 1930. In his later years, Brown ran a dude ranch in the Icicle Valley.

Hikers, including members of organized clubs such as The Mountaineers, Mazamas, and the Cascadians, have been enjoying the Stevens Pass area since the early 1900s. The Mountaineers Club was organized in 1906, promoted by physician C. E. Eaton, and endorsed by Edward Curtis, the famous photographer of Indians. The club's first three annual trips were to the Olympic Mountains, the top of Mount Adams, and the top of Mount Rainier, respectively. On the fourth outing, in 1910, The Mountaineers chose to scale Glacier Peak.

Sixty-nine members of the Seattle Mountaineers Club left the GNR train at Nason Creek on July 23, 1910, and headed for the peak. The climbers included writers and artists from the East Coast. Each person was permitted thirty-five pounds of luggage, which was carried by a pack train that also hauled in the food and utensils. With little or no direct trail northward, they bushwhacked their way via the Chiwawa River, a tributary of the Wenatchee River, to its junction with Buck Creek. From there most of the party, thirty-seven women and thirty-two men, ascended Glacier Peak. One climber said that, as the party looked down from the peak, a blanket of clouds obscured the lower levels, cutting off some of the higher peaks and making them look like jagged teeth. From Buck Creek Pass, the party descended to the head of Lake Chelan, then followed the lake to the Columbia River, where they took the steamer *Columbia* to Wenatchee. There they were entertained at lunch by the Wenatchee Commercial Club.

The Mountaineers came to the Stevens Pass area again on June 15, 1914, this time starting from Leavenworth to make their way up Mount Stuart. The party went up Icicle River to Eight Mile Creek, following the latter to a high valley to make camp for the ascent. Afterward they trekked over to Chiwaukum to catch the train for Seattle. Three years later a large party returned to climb Glacier Peak again, by the same route used in 1910.

Mazamas of Portland climbed Glacier Peak and hiked to Lake Chelan in August 1926, essentially along the same route The Mountaineers had followed. The cost of the two-week 1926 outing was $75, less railroad fare if one started from Leavenworth. Mazamas, a climbing and outdoors club, was organized at the summit of Mount Hood in 1894; membership was limited to those who had climbed to the summit of a perpetually snowcapped mountain that had at least one glacier attainable only by foot. By 1926, the group had almost a thousand members.

The Cascadians, a Yakima climbing club, climbed Mount Stuart in the Ingalls Creek area each Memorial Day. Charley Cockburn, a bank cashier from Lake Stevens, recalled the climb in a June 12, 1936, *Echo* article. At the time of the trip, one could drive to Ingalls Creek Lodge, where the eleven-mile trail for the climbing camp began. The twenty-eight-member party was entertained that night by a "terrific electrical storm, lighting the peaks with sheets of lightning and with thunder like the crack of doom. It rained hardly at all, much to our relief. . . ."

The party was on the trail by 5:30 A.M. and stopped for lunch in the saddle below the "false peak." As the climbers ascended, they soon could see Mount Rainier and Mount Adams, then the Puget Sound country "with tongues of cloud running up the valley." On the south side of Ingalls Creek, the mountains were of volcanic origin, covered by cinders, with no growth. To the north was granite. "Directly opposite us was a peak with a balanced rock on it, probably 30 or 40 feet high, which sways perceptibly with the wind." The party began the final climb roped together, since the ridge had a sharp drop-off. At the summit, the view included the whole length of Eight Mile Creek to its junction with the Icicle. On the way down, a climber slipped; the other three in her party flattened themselves and slid a short distance, but the anchoring stopped her dangerous trip. Cockburn later reminisced about the "fine trip and a fine time."

Mountain people witnessed odd happenings in the Stevens Pass area. In July 1912, sheepman C. M. Snow reported that the jagged peak of Mount Ingalls had split in two and fallen into the canyon below and into Icicle Lake. Immense boulders blocked the trail up the mountain. Astonished listeners attributed the phenomenon to an Alaskan earthquake that had occurred about that time. In 1920, many spectators witnessed the collapse of Round Mountain near Lake Wenatchee when part of it broke loose and crashed down, sending up a huge dust cloud. Witnesses three miles away felt the jolt.

In the 1920s and 1930s, bears were numerous in the Ingalls and Icicle area. A hiker reported encountering thirteen bears in a fifteen-mile trip; once he narrowly escaped from a mother bear defending her cubs against the hiker's dog. The dog turned tail and, pursued by mama, ran right to his master, who had the presence of mind to beat a spoon furiously on a cooking pan. In the Chumstick Valley, a Civilian Conservation Corps group building roads was supervised by a virtual herd of curious bears. There were few problems, however, with the black bears common to the Cascades. There were only very occasional sightings of grizzlies who may have wandered into the northern Cascades from Canada.

As part of the effort to protect wildlife, the state of Washington founded a state fish hatchery program in 1896. In 1914, the state began maintaining a small hatchery near Leavenworth. In 1937, plans were set in motion to build the "world's largest salmon hatchery" at the junction of the Wenatchee and Icicle rivers, the ancient fishing grounds of the Wenatchi Indians. Building the hatchery was a response to the dwindling numbers of salmon in the Columbia River, a problem that is still being addressed today. Fish counts at the Rock Island Dam below Wenatchee revealed that less than 17,000 of the expected 40,000 blueback salmon had passed that point in 1938; in 1935 and 1936, silver salmon were almost nonexistent. The situation was expected to become worse upon completion of Grand Coulee Dam, although some "experts" asserted that only a small percentage of the salmon swam beyond the site of Grand Coulee.

In a combined effort of the U.S. Bureau of Reclamation, state and federal fisheries, and others, the engineering and construction of the hatchery was largely completed by 1940. It is still operating vigorously today. Although the state lobbied to manage the hatchery, it remains a federal installation.

The plan was to intercept spawning salmon at Rock Island and truck them in controlled-environment tank trucks to the Wenatchee River, where they could make their way upriver on their own. The project included auxiliary rearing systems in the Entiat and other rivers north of the Wenatchee. As the fish entered the holding ponds at Leavenworth, they were milked of eggs, which were then hatched and the young salmon reared until they were ready to be released to make their pilgrimage to the ocean and back.

The specifications for the original system were quite detailed. Salmon would enter from the river into two parallel holding ponds 200 feet wide and 2,000 feet long. Then came 48 standard "picking troughs," each 30 feet long, and 768 standard hatchery troughs, each 15 feet long. After the eggs were milked from the salmon, they were placed in 96 deep troughs for hatching, each 30 feet long. The hatched fry went into one of 100 concrete primary rearing ponds, then progressed to 110 natural-type secondary rearing ponds.

A water diversion system to provide a controlled supply of clean water was built. Part of the water was made available through the 1938–39 construction of a 2,500-foot diversion tunnel from Snow Lake into Icicle Creek, intended to augment the supply of water in the creek during the arid summer months. The tunnel began at or under Snow Lake and was fed by the nearby Nada Lake as well. The construction was a remarkable feat. Before work could begin, an adequate trail for pack animals had to be built; it opened on October 17, 1938. Some supplies were dropped from aircraft. A camp at Nada Lake consisted of dormitories, a mess hall, a cook shack, a compressor house, a blacksmith shop, a powder shed, and other facilities. Contact from this wilderness area to Leavenworth was maintained by shortwave radio.

The 2,500-foot tunnel was started about 200 feet below the surface of Snow Lake and was blasted out at a gradual incline to intercept the bottom of the lake. Little or no timbering was required for the five-by-seven-foot tunnel, because it went through virtually solid granite. Once completed, the lake's output was governed by a large-gate valve that, when opened, sent water surging through the tunnel to vent and run down a slope into Icicle Creek. The addition of this cold, fresh water was needed only about one month of each year in late summer, to bolster the flow in Icicle Creek and into the hatchery at a crucial time in the salmon's life cycle. During their arduous trip upstream to spawn, salmon incur skin abrasions that can easily become infected by bacteria or fungus; the cold water inhibits such infections.

The main hatchery building measured 225 by 88 feet and had two additional wings of 36 by 45 feet. There was space for administration and storage. The building construction contract was awarded to the MacDonald Construction Co. of Seattle, and the building was completed at a cost of $94,000. About a hundred men gained employment on the overall project. An old log cabin on the site was enlarged to provide a dormitory for about twenty men.

The work was done largely under the supervision of Frank Banks, Grand Coulee construction engineer; the first valve was opened and tested on October 26, 1939. In 1939 and 1940, a three-mile canal was built to control water entering the hatchery from the Wenatchee River as well. This was soon abandoned because the water was too warm.

When of sufficient maturity, the young fry were placed in the various streams from Rock Island Dam north to Grand Coulee. From there the salmon went downstream, eventually returning to those streams to spawn naturally. Their trips from the hatchery to the high lakes and remote streams were made in tanks on the backs of packhorses. About 700,000 fingerlings were released in August 1940, with another 200,000 released in September or October of that year.

The historic hatchery continues its work today. The established salmon now make their way upstream without assistance, some coming into the main hatchery for milking. In 1993, the hatchery released 1.7 million yearling smolts.

Afterword

One by one, the railroad camps and lumber villages disappeared, or almost so; only Leavenworth, Skykomish, and Index remain viable towns today. After being brought up to state-highway standards, Stevens Pass Highway has undergone regular upgrades; it now has passing lanes on many two-lane sections and divided roads along the steeper grades.

The tortuous curves of the old highway west of the summit, much of it one lane wide with turnouts for passing, were replaced by a new section of road between the summit of Stevens Pass and Scenic, on which construction began in the mid-1930s. The highway was open year-round for the first time in 1942, and by 1950, the highway was paved or oiled from Wenatchee to Everett.

The fortieth anniversary of the first time a car *reached* Stevens Pass, in 1923 (as opposed to the first time a car *crossed* the pass, which was in 1924), was celebrated on March 3, 1963, as Governor Albert D. Rosellini snipped a ribbon to open a new four-lane segment of the highway on the west side of the pass, a further improvement. Warning lights for traction tires or chains, regular snowplow runs, and frequent monitoring by road personnel make the highway an all-year thoroughfare these days, with perhaps the majority of cars recreation-bound.

Along Stevens Pass today, the presence of the Burlington Northern Railroad (formed by the 1970 merger of the Great Northern Railway with several other railroads) is indicated only by the trains that pass through the area; there are no depots. The section from Wenatchee to Everett is under the management of the Cascade Division at Everett. Fortunately, the Eight-Mile Tunnel has eliminated most of the terrible snow-related accidents that plagued the line during the GNR's first decades in the Cascades.

Accidents still happen, though. A particularly tragic disaster struck Stevens Pass on January 24, 1971. Slides covered parts of the highway both east and west of the pass with fifty to sixty feet of snow. Then a major avalanche thundered down Mount Lichtenberg to overwhelm the Yodelin settlement, just east of the pass. The size of a football field, the slide slammed into cabins whose occupants lay sleeping. Four people were killed in two cabins: Barton and Nancy Edgers, twelve-year-old

Peggy Dean, and young Kenneth Lewis. Eleven other members of three families survived. Verl Lyon, the driver of a front-loader attempting to clear the west-side pass road, was injured when his rig was shoved sideways by still another avalanche and smashed against a guardrail; had the rail failed, Lyon would have dropped into a canyon.

With clear hindsight the authorities declared that the Yodelin development and ski area should never have been built because the site was a known slide area. Today harmful avalanches are ever more rare, because trained crews analyze and destroy potential slides harmlessly by using special guns to trigger them—both along the highway and on the ski slopes.

Windy Point/Skyline Ridge spawns avalanches almost every year, most relatively harmless because the railroad has moved. In the 1970s, however, a large slide carried a railroad bridge near Scenic 400 to 500 feet to fetch up beside Highway 2. A major avalanche came off Skyline Ridge in 1990, in the same general area as the Wellington slide of 1910, taking down a half mile of Puget Power's lines and six sets of power poles as well as slicing down timber as large as twenty-four inches in diameter.

While the Wenatchee and Skykomish rivers once were filled with plunging logs destined for mills, they now are traveled by river rafters. The Skykomish trips start at Index; the Wenatchee trips go either from Lake Wenatchee to Tumwater Canyon, or from Leavenworth downstream to Cashmere or Monitor. Most do not run Tumwater Canyon because parts of the canyon are Class 6 whitewater, a designation of greater challenge than most rafters are willing to risk.

Individuals, independent groups, and organized hiking clubs such as The Mountaineers and Mazamas enjoy climbing the surrounding mountains. Both the Index area and Icicle Valley are considered tops, with experts calling the Mount Stuart Range one of the best and most varied alpine climbing areas around. As part of the club's 1977 advanced rock climbing program, Mazamas came to Leavenworth during the Memorial Day holidays. As a warm-up they climbed the Peshastin Pinnacles, an eroded sandstone area that looks like a miniature Bryce Canyon. The climbers then attacked Snow Creek Wall, first explored by The Mountaineers' Fred Beckey in the 1960s. Lou Lauman of the Mazama party described his exhilaration in a club newsmagazine: "I belong here. For me, climbing Orbit [on Snow Creek Wall] is a celebration in linking the body, the mind, the rock into a cohesive unit. Nothing is in opposition. Seldom have I felt so alive. Seldom have I experienced such joy." The group also climbed Outer Space, in the area, and Castle Rock, near Leavenworth.

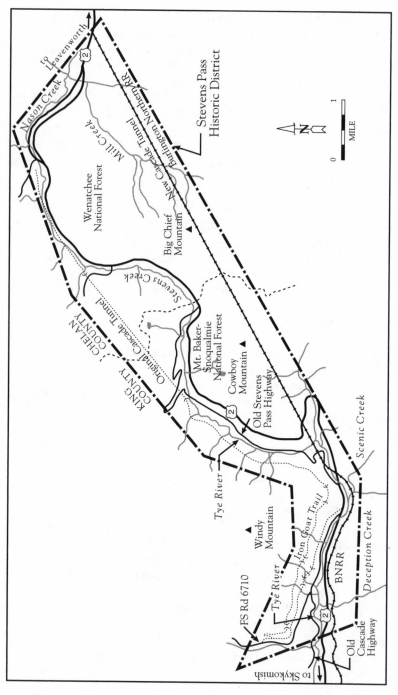

Downhill skiing, snowboarding, and cross-country skiing are very popular at Stevens Pass today, all monitored by a USFS "snow ranger" who lives right at the pass. An ever-growing industry of the upper Wenatchee and Icicle Valleys caters to cross-country skiers, who often hole up at the small valley lodges that offer après-ski activities such as sleigh rides.

The exciting past of Stevens Pass led to its consideration as a historic site as early as August 25, 1969. The brainchild of Washington State University archaeologist Harvey Rice and many others, the idea took root: an eight-square-mile area, encompassing the original switchbacks and both the old and new Cascade tunnels, was studied. The Stevens Pass Historic District was added to the National Register of Historic Places on December 7, 1976. It runs roughly from Martin Creek to the east portal of the Cascade Tunnel (as the Eight-Mile Tunnel is now called).

Today a car can roll comfortably through Stevens Pass from Index to Leavenworth or Cashmere in a couple of hours. There seems little to see except trees and mountains, albeit beautiful ones. Yet on the dirt lanes and portions of original highway, on the trails following discarded rail beds, listen hard and look keenly. You might sense the ghosts of the hundreds of workers and their families who once sweated and froze, laughed, cried, gave birth, and died in those crossroads communities and camps of Stevens Pass.

Bibliography

Anderson, Eva. *Rails Across the Cascades*. Wenatchee, Wash.: World Publishing Co., 1980.

Bauhof, Frederick C. "Construction History of the Cascade Railroad Tunnel." *Engineering Geology in Washington, Vol. 2.* Washington Division of Geology and Earth Resources Bulletin No. 78, 1989.

Baxter, J. C., D. J. Kerr, and Frederick Mears. "The Eight-Mile Cascade Tunnel: Great Northern Railway." American Society of Civil Engineers Symposium, February 1931.

Beckey, Fred. *Cascade Alpine Guide*. 2d ed. Seattle: The Mountaineers, 1989.

Bogue, V. G. "Reports on surveys April 25, 1882, Engineer for the Cascade Division, Northern Pacific Railroad." Collection of Lloyd Berry.

Buntain, Alpha Burgess. *They Found a Valley*. Plain, Wash.: Alpha Burgess Buntain, 1986.

Burgstahler, Ruth. *Index*. Index, Wash.: Ruth Burgstahler, 1979.

Chapple, Oliver. "Avalanche in the Cascades." *The American West*, January/February 1983.

Clark, Donald H. *18 Men and a Horse*. Bellingham, Wash.: Whatcom Museum of History and Art, 1969.

The Coast, December 1903, March 1905, July 1906, November 1906, and November 1908.

"Concrete and Timber Showsheds on the Great Northern R[ailwa]y." *Engineering News*, December 15, 1910.

Doty, James, Secretary. *Journal of Operations of Governor Isaac Ingalls Stevens of Washington Territory in 1855*. Edited by Edward J. Kowrach. Veradale, Wash.: Edward J. Kowrach, 1978.

Dow, Edson. *Passes to the North*. Wenatchee, Wash.: Edson Dow, 1963.

Eckman, Leonard Clarence. "The Geography of Occupance in the Skykomish Valley." Master's thesis, University of Washington, 1937.

"Extensive Great Northern Snow Shed Construction." *Railway Age*, April 17, 1914.

Galm, Jerry R., and Ruth A. Masten. *Avey's Orchard: Archaeological*

Investigation of a Late Prehistoric Columbia River Community. Cheney, Wash.: Eastern Washington University Reports in Archaeology and History, 1985.

Gellatly, John A. *History of Wenatchee.* Wenatchee, Wash. [1962?]

Gray, William R. *The Pacific Crest Trail.* Washington, D.C.: National Geographic Society, 1975.

Guie, H. Dean. *Bugles in the Valley.* Yakima, Wash.: H. Dean Guie, 1956.

Hartranft, W. C. "The First Cascade Tunnel." Great Northern Railway Historical Society, Reference Sheet No. 175, March 1991.

———. "The Pacific Extension and Cascade Switchbacks 1889–1892." Great Northern Railway Historical Society, Reference Sheet No. 172, December 1990.

Haskell, Daniel C., ed. "On Reconnaissance for the Great Northern, Letters of C. F. B. Haskell, 1889–1891." *Bulletin of the New York Library,* February 1948 and March 1948.

The Head Saw (Bloedel Donovan Lumber Mills newsletter). Selected issues, 1923 and 1924. Deming Log Show Museum.

Hidy, Ralph Willard. *The Great Northern Railway History.* Boston: Harvard Business School, 1988.

Hodges, L. K. *Mining in the Pacific Northwest.* Seattle: The Post Intelligencer, 1897.

Hoggson, Noble. *A Biography of Horace Chapin Henry, 1844–1928.* Seattle: Langdon C. Henry, 1960.

Horr, David Agee, ed. *American Indian Ethnohistory.* New York: Garland Publishing Inc., 1974.

Hull, Lindley M., ed. *History of Central Washington.* Spokane, Wash.: Pioneer Historical Association of Central Washington, 1929.

Hult, Ruby El. *Northwest Disaster: Avalanche and Fire.* Portland, Ore. Binfords & Mort, 1960.

Illustrated History of the Big Bend Country. Spokane, Wash.: Western Historical Publishing Co., 1904.

Inkster, Tom H. "John Frank Stevens, American Engineer." *Pacific Northwest Quarterly,* April 1965.

Intlekofer, Charles F. "Railroad Construction in Stevens Pass." *Confluence* (publication of the North Central Washington Museum), Summer 1992.

Kappler, Charles J., ed. *Indian Affairs, Laws and Treaties,* Vol. 1. 1904–41. Reprint. New York: AMS Press, 1971.

Kelly, Plympton J. *We Were Not Summer Soldiers: The Indian War Diary of Plympton J. Kelly.* Introduction and annotations by William N. Bischoff. Tacoma, Wash.: Washington State Historical Society, 1976.

Kerr, Charles C. *The World of the World*. Wenatchee, Wash.: Wenatchee World, 1980.

Lambrecht, Frank, and Dora Lambrecht. "Bavaria in the Cascades." *American West*, October 1988.

Landes, Henry. *Washington Geological Survey*, Vol. 2. Olympia, Wash.: State of Washington, 1903.

Lauman, Lou. "Fun in the Sun with the Mazama Rock Climbing Program," *Mazama*, 1977.

Leavenworth Ranger Station. "Cady Pass." Letter from Norman Lenfest, January 21, 1974.

———. Copy of letter from Wayne L. Bostwick to Bernice Green, November 1, 1974.

———. Text for slide show by Dennis McMillin. 1993.

———. Lily Holm scrapbook.

———. "The Location of the Great Northern Railroad." Undated typescript.

Lewis, Darin. "Mining in the Red Mountain Area." *Confluence* (publication of the North Central Washington Museum), Fall 1984.

Linsley, D. C. "Pioneering in the Cascade Country." *Civil Engineering*, June 1932.

———. "A Railroad Survey of the Sauk and Wenatchee Rivers in 1870." *Northwest Discovery*, April 1981.

MacKay, Donald. *Empire of Wood*. Vancouver, B.C.: Douglas & McIntyre, 1982.

Martin, Albro. *James Jerome Hill*. New York: Oxford University Press, 1976.

Mitchell, Bruce. *By River, Trail and Rail*. Wenatchee, Wash.: Wenatchee Daily World, 1968.

Moltke, Alfred W. *Memoirs of a Logger*. College Place, Wash.: Alfred W. Moltke, 1965.

Mount Baker–Snoqualmie National Forest Archives, Mountlake Terrace, Wash. "Cascade Crest Trail, Miles 198–329." Pamphlet. August and September 1935.

———. "A Cultural Resource Overview: Prehistory, Ethnography and History." Report by Jan L. Hollenbeck. August 1987.

———. "High Road to a Wild Paradise." Undated excerpt from magazine article by Robert Cantwell.

National Archives, Resources Division, Washington, D.C. "Excerpts from Council on Yakima Agency on the Matter of Selling the Wenatchi Indian Fishery Reservation, December 18 and 19, 1893," by John Hamilt [*sic*]. (Copy in Indian History file at Wenatchee Public Library.)

National Archives, War Records Division, Washington, D.C. "Camp on the Wenatcha River," letter from George Wright to Jones (first name unknown), July 7, 1856.

Nicandri, David L. *Northwest Chiefs*. Tacoma, Wash.: Washington State Historical Society, 1986.

Nielsen, Carl J. "The Snow Lake Tunnel: Migratory Fish Control, Columbia Basin Project." *The Reclamation Era*, March 1940.

Patty, E. N. "Metal Mines of Washington." *Washington State Geological Survey Bulletin No. 23*, 1921.

Pioneers Committee. *An Illustrated History of Skagit and Snohomish Counties*. Interstate Publishing Company, 1906.

Pollard, Lancaster. *A History of the State of Washington*, Vol. 3. Portland, Ore.: Binfords & Mort, 1941.

Ray, Verne F. "Ethnohistorical Notes on the Columbia, Chelan, Entiat, and Wenatchee Tribes." In *Interior Salish and Eastern Washington Indians IV*. New York: Garland Publishing Inc., 1974.

Roe, JoAnn. *The Columbia River*. Golden, Colo.: Fulcrum Publishing, 1992.

———. *The North Cascadians*. Seattle: Madrona Press, 1980.

Rogers, A. B. Diary, 1887. Transcribed by Emily Rogers Valentine. Manuscripts and University Archives Division, University of Washington Libraries, Seattle.

Rogers, Chris. "The History of the Icicle Irrigation District." Unpublished manuscript, 1962. Collection of Elaine Berry.

Ruby, Robert H., and John A. Brown. *Half-Sun on the Columbia*. Norman, Okla.: University of Oklahoma Press, 1965.

———. *Indians of the Pacific Northwest*. Norman, Okla.: University of Oklahoma Press, 1981.

"Scenic Hot Springs." *The Seattle Mail and Herald*, August 4, 1906.

"Scenic Hot Springs." *The Town Crier* (Northwest weekly arts magazine), January 22, 1921.

Scheuerman, Richard D., ed. *The Wenatchi Indians: Guardians of the Valley*. Cashmere, Wash.: Cashmere Public Schools, 1982. (Reprinted by Ye Galleon Press, Fairfield, Wash.)

Schmitt, Martin F. *General George Crook*. Norman, Okla.: University of Oklahoma Press, 1946.

Skykomish Ranger Station. Letter from Carrie Starr Weismann, March 6, 1928.

———. Letter from George Flanagan to F. W. Cleator, January 3, 1934.

———. "Cultural Resource Narrative Reports (including report by Joan Peter)," September 24, 1979.

———. Undated excerpt from *Compressed Air Magazine*.

Spring, Ira, and Byron Fish. *Lookouts*. Seattle: The Mountaineers, 1981.

Steele, Richard F. *Illustrated History of Stevens, Ferry, Okanogan and Chelan Counties*. Spokane, Wash.: Western History Publishing Co., 1904.

Stevens, John F. *An Engineer's Recollections*. New York: McGraw Hill Publishing Co., Inc., 1936.

————. "Great Northern Railway." *Washington Historical Quarterly*, April 1929.

"Stone Works Industry Flourished in Index." *Everett Herald*, June 29, 1976.

Strawn, Charles. "Switch Backs to Diesel Locomotives . . . The Great Northern Railroad." *Confluence* (publication of the North Central Washington Museum), Fall 1984.

Streamer, Francis. Miscellaneous diaries, letters, and notes. Washington State Library, Olympia, Wash. Microfilm.

"Sunset Mine Stages a Comeback." *Washingtonian*, November 1928.

"Surveys of the Skagit [Linsley's Pass] and Skykomish and Ward's Pass and Route," Engineer's Office, Portland, Ore. (includes notes and letters by Thomas B. Morris, engineer for the Northern Pacific Railroad). Collection of Lloyd Berry, Wenatchee, Wash.

"Turn Back to the Index." *Everett Herald*, November 23, 1977.

Tweddell, Colin Ellidge. "A Historical and Ethnological Study of the Snohomish Indian People." August 1953. U.S. Forest Service Regional Archives, Seattle.

U.S. Department of Agriculture. "100 Years of Federal Forestry." *Agricultural Information Bulletin No. 402*, December 1976.

U.S. Forest Service. *Stevens Pass Historic District: Historic Resource Management Plan*. 1988/1989.

Washington Atlas & Gazetteer. Freeport, Maine: DeLorme Mapping Company, 1988.

Washington Magazine. Excerpt from untitled article about Scenic Hot Springs. July 1906.

Wenatchee Public Library. "The Upper Wenatchee Valley." Brochure. Circa 1910.

————. Letter from Moses George to Bernice Green, January 20, 1975.

————. Notes from interviews 1978–80 with Joseph Atkins about White River encounter.

————. "History of Blewett Mining District, Chelan County, Washington." Typescript by Daniel Y. Meschter. 1980.

————. "The Geological Story of Central Washington." Undated typescript by Otis W. Freeman. Eastern Washington College of Education.

White, Victor. "Brakeman on the Great Northern," *Frontier Times*, September 1970.

Whitfield, William, ed. *History of Snohomish County*, Vols. 1 and 2. Chicago: Pioneer Historical Publishing Company, 1926.

Wing, Robert C., ed. *A Century of Service*. Bellevue, Wash.: Puget Sound Power & Light Company, 1987.

Wolfe, P. B., ed. *Wolfe's History of Clinton, Iowa*, Vol. 1. Indianapolis: B. F. Bowen & Co., 1911.

Wood, C. E. S. *Century Magazine*, New Series, November 1886–April 1887.

Woodhouse, Philip R. *Monte Cristo*. Seattle: The Mountaineers, 1979.

Wood, Charles, and Dorothy Wood. *The Great Northern Railway*. Edmonds, Wash.: Pacific Fast Mail, 1979.

Wood, Charles R. *Lines West*. New York: Bonanza Books, n.d.

Selected editions of the following newspapers: *Cashmere Valley Record, Everett Herald, Index Miner, Index News, Leavenworth Echo, Seattle Post-Intelligencer, Seattle Times,* and *Wenatchee World.*

Index

JoAnn Roe has lived in the western United States all of her adult life, first in California, then in Washington. She has published numerous magazine articles, in both national and regional magazines, and is the author of eight books, including *The Columbia River: A Historical Travel Guide*, *Frank Matsura: Frontier Photographer*, which won the Pacific Northwest Booksellers Award for Literary Excellence and the state of Washington's Governor's Writers Award, and the *Marco the Manx* series of books for children. She is a member of the Pacific Northwest Historians Guild and Western Writers of America.

THE MOUNTAINEERS, founded in 1906, is a nonprofit outdoor activity and conservation club, whose mission is "to explore, study, preserve, and enjoy the natural beauty of the outdoors. . . ." Based in Seattle, Washington, the club is now the third-largest such organization in the United States, with 15,000 members and four branches throughout Washington state.

The Mountaineers sponsors both classes and year-round outdoor activities in the Pacific Northwest, which include hiking, mountain climbing, ski-touring, snowshoeing, bicycling, camping, kayaking and canoeing, nature study, sailing, and adventure travel. The club's conservation division supports environmental causes through educational activities, sponsoring legislation, and presenting informational programs. All club activities are led by skilled, experienced volunteers, who are dedicated to promoting safe and responsible enjoyment and preservation of the outdoors.

The Mountaineers Books, an active, nonprofit publishing program of the club, produces guidebooks, instructional texts, historical works, natural history guides, and works on environmental conservation. All books produced by The Mountaineers are aimed at fulfilling the club's mission.

If you would like to participate in these organized outdoor activities or the club's programs, consider a membership in The Mountaineers. For information and an application, write or call The Mountaineers, Club Headquarters, 300 Third Avenue West, Seattle, Washington 98119; (206) 284-6310.

Send or call for our catalog of more than 300 outdoor titles:
The Mountaineers Books
1011 SW Klickitat Way, Suite 107
Seattle, WA 98134
1-800-553-4453